Katherine Anderson is a very experienced barrister and education law specialist ranked as a Leading Junior in Chambers and Partners and Legal 500 rankings since 2021. She regularly acts in proceedings before the First-tier Tribunal and Upper Tribunal on behalf of parents, young people, local authorities, and responsible bodies for schools. Her own education was at Cambridge University, United Kingdom, and Harvard University, United States. She is a member of 3PB Barristers, described by The Legal 500 2021 as a set that is "increasingly becoming a powerhouse in education law".

A Practical Guide to Education, Health and Care Plan Appeals in England

A Practical Guide to Education, Health and Care Plan Appeals in England

Katherine Anderson

Law Brief Publishing

The information in this book was believed to be correct at the time of writing. All content is for information purposes only and is not intended as legal advice. No liability is accepted by either the publisher or author for any errors or omissions (whether negligent or not) that it may contain. Professional advice should always be obtained before applying any information to particular circumstances.

Published 2023 by Law Brief Publishing, an imprint of Law Brief Publishing Ltd
30 The Parks
Minehead
Somerset
TA24 8BT

www.lawbriefpublishing.com

Paperback: 978-1-913715-34-2

PREFACE

According to Ministry of Justice statistics, in the academic year 2021/22, HMCTS tribunals recorded 11,000 registered 'SEN' appeals, an increase of 29% when compared to the prior year. Most likely this state of affairs does not reflect the vision which was set out in the forward to the 2015 statutory guidance, 'Special educational needs and disability code of practice: 0 to 25 years', of a system which is 'less confrontational and more efficient'. This book is aimed as a practical guide for lawyers who are representing parties in 'SEN' appeals: young people with special educational needs, the parents of children with SEN, or local authorities. Its aims are to explain the relevant law as it has developed under the current and previous statutory regimes and the practice and procedure of the First-tier Tribunal (Special Educational Needs and Disability), and to help parties' representatives to help the Tribunal to deal with these cases fairly and justly. The vision for children and young people with special educational needs, set out in the forward to the Code of Practice, that they achieve well in their early years, at school and in college, and lead happy and fulfilled lives, is one which all can share. This book is dedicated to those children and young people, and to everyone who is working to improve educational support for them.

I would like to thank Law Brief Publishing Ltd for the opportunity to write this book, my 'powerhouse' of colleagues and clerks in the Education Law team at 3PB Barristers, and my family.

This book reflects the state of the law as understood by me on 17 March 2023.

Katherine Anderson
March 2023

CONTENTS

CHAPTER ONE

OVERVIEW

Introduction

Parents and young people have a right to appeal to the First-tier Tribunal (Special Educational Needs and Disability) against certain decisions made by local authorities in England relating to children's and young persons' EHC needs assessments and EHC plans (a 'young person' in this context is a person over compulsory school age and under 25). This right to appeal is afforded by section 51 of the Children and Families Act 2014, Part 3. The First-tier Tribunal (SEND) forms part of the First-tier Tribunal (Health, Educational and Social Care Chamber) overseen by His Majesty's Courts and Tribunals service. The key legislation which governs this type of appeal is to be found in Part 3 of the 2014 Act, in various provisions of the Education Act 1996, in the Special Educational Needs and Disability Regulations 2014, made under the 2014 Act, as well as in the Special Educational Needs and Disability (First-tier Tribunal Recommendations Power) Regulations 2017, relating to 'extended appeals'. Statutory guidance issued by the Department for Education and Department of Health under section 77 of the 2014 Act – the Special Educational Needs and Disability Code of Practice: 0 to 25 years ("the SEND Code of Practice") – is also key.

An "EHC needs assessment" is an assessment of the educational, health care and social care needs of a child or young person, defined under section 36 of the 2014 Act. EHC needs assessments are explained further in Chapter 2 of this book. An "EHC plan" is a plan defined under section 37. It specifies the child's or young person's special educational needs ('SEN') and the special educational provision required by him or her, as well as, *inter alia*, any health care provision and social care provision reasonably required by the learning difficulties and disabilities which result in the child or young person having SEN and, in the case of a child or a young person aged under 18, any social care provision which must be made for him or her by the relevant local authority as a result of section 2 of the Chronically Sick and Disabled Persons Act 1970. It will also, usually, name the school, maintained nursery school, post-16 institution or other institution to be attended by the child or young person and/or the type of school or institution. The form of an EHC plan is prescribed by regulation 12 of the 2014 Regulations. There must be eleven sections, labelled A-K. For example, section B sets out the child or young person's SEN, while section F sets out the special educational provision which the child or young person requires. EHC plans are explained further in Chapter 3 of this book.

"Special educational needs" is defined under section 20 of the 2014 Act. Special educational provision" is defined under section 21 of that Act. These definitions are explained further in Chapters 4 and 5.

Under the scheme provided for by the 2014 Act, most children and young people with special educational needs should have their needs met within local mainstream early years settings, schools or colleges, without an EHC plan. However, if an EHC plan is made, the child or young person enters a world of specific educational entitlements that are not enjoyed by other children or young people. An EHC plan provides a significant degree of certainty and stability in educational provision.

There are six types of appeal that a child's parent or a young person may bring to the First-tier Tribunal under section 51 of the 2014 Act. The first type of appeal is against the decision of a local authority not to secure an EHC needs assessment for the child or young person: this may be referred to as a 'refusal to assess' appeal. This type of appeal is explained in Chapter 2 of this book. The second type of appeal is against a decision of a local authority, following an EHC needs assessment, that it is not necessary for special educational provision to be made for the child or young person in accordance with an EHC plan: a 'refusal to issue' appeal. This type of appeal is explained in Chapter 3. Where an EHC plan is maintained for the child or young person, the child's parent or a young person can appeal the child's or young person's SEN as specified in the plan and/or the special educational provision specified in the plan and/or the school or other institution named in the plan or the type of school or other institution specified in the plan, or, if no school or other institution is named in the plan, that fact. As these are the matters which are set out in sections B, F and I of the EHC plan, they may be referred to as 'Section B' and 'F' and 'I' appeals. These types of appeals are explained in Chapters 4 to 6. Chapter 5, on 'Section F' appeals, includes an explanation of the law relating to educational provision outside of the normal school day, sometimes referred to as a 'waking day curriculum'. Chapter 7 addresses the special situation provided for by section 61 of the 2014 Act, whereby special educational provision may be made otherwise than in a school or post-16 institution or a place at which relevant early years education is provided. This is type of provision is sometimes referred to by the shorthand 'EOTAS'.

The fourth type of appeal is against a decision of a local authority not to secure a re-assessment of the needs of the child or young person under section 44 of the 2014 Act, following a request to do so; this type of appeal, a 'refusal to re-assess' appeal, is explained in Chapter 2. The fifth type of appeal is against a decision of a LA not to secure the amendment or replacement of an EHC plan it maintains for the child or young person following a review or re-assessment under section 44 of the 2014 Act; this is a type of 'Section B', 'F' or "I' appeal and is explained in Chapters 4 to 6. The sixth type of appeal is against a decision of a LA under section 45 of the 2014 Act, to cease to maintain an EHC plan for the child or young person: a 'ceasing to maintain' appeal. This type of appeal is explained in Chapter 8.

Chapter 9 of this book explains the legal framework whereby local authorities and health care bodies are required to make joint commissioning arrangements for education, health and care provision for children and young people with SEN or disabilities. It further explains the involvement of local authority children's and adults' social care services and health care bodies in EHC needs and assessments, and the powers conferred on the First-Tier Tribunal by the Special Educational Needs and Disability (First-tier Tribunal Recommendations Power) Regulations 2017. Under these regulations parents and young people can request, and the Tribunal can make, non-binding recommendations about health and social care needs or provision as part of any of the six types of appeal referred to above, except for the first type ('refusal to assess' appeals). Since 1 September 2021 appeals which include health or social care aspects have been known as 'extended appeals'.

Chapters 2 to 9 of this book also address the powers of the First-tier Tribunal before determining and when determining these types of appeal, as well as compliance with the Tribunal's orders.

There is no right of appeal to the First-tier Tribunal in relation the other sections of an EHC plan. However, the Tribunal has a power to make "any other consequential amendments as [it] thinks fit" to the EHC plan, by virtue of regulation 42(2)(f) of the 2014 regulations. In *S v Worcestershire CC (SEN)* [2017] UKUT 0092 (AAC) at [84-85], in the context of a 'Section F' appeal, the Upper Tribunal held that this meant the Tribunal could make consequential amendments to the outcomes stated in Section E.

Practice and procedure in the First-tier Tribunal, in relation to these types of appeals, is explained in Chapter 10 of this book. This Chapter briefly explains the 'mediation' requirement. It also addresses the situation where one parent of a child brings an appeal without the other, and the situation where a young person lacks capacity to bring an appeal.

Correcting, setting aside, reviewing and appealing First-tier Tribunal decisions is looked at in Chapter 11.

Part 3 of the Children and Families Act 2014 and the Education Act 1996 – overview

Part 3 of the 2014 Act makes provision for children and young people <u>in England</u> with SEN or disabilities. Part 3 of the 2014 Act made various changes to the previous statutory regime. Of these changes, arguably the most significant was the introduction of EHC plans which can be maintained for children and young people of any age from 0-25 years, to replace statements of special educational needs. In addition, section 81 of the 2014 Act caused the provisions of Chapter 1 of Part 4 of the

Education Act 1996 to cease to apply in relation to children in the area of a local authority in England. The effect was to create a new statutory regime for England and a separate statutory scheme for Wales. Some of the case law decided in relation to the sections of the Education Act 1996 which no longer apply to England continues to be relevant. In *Devon County Council v OH* [2016] UKUT 292 (AAC) at [30-32] the Upper Tribunal noted "substantially common features around the very building blocks of the special educational needs regime" and, at [33], decided to "proceed on the basis that the legislative intention was in general terms for a continuity of approach, except where the 2014 Act provides a specific reason to conclude otherwise. Subject to that note of caution, authorities on concepts common to both regimes will continue to be relevant."

Section 83 of the 2014 Act deals with interpretation of Part 3. By section 83(7), the Education Act 1996 and the other provisions of Part 3 of the 2014 (except so far as they amend other Acts) are to be read as if those provisions were contained in the 1996 Act.

The 1996 Act remains a key piece of legislation for England in the context of appeals to the First-tier Tribunal under section 51 of the 2014 Act. In particular:

- Section 2 defines primary, secondary and further education.

- Section 3 defines "pupil".

- Section 4 defines schools and section 5 defines primary schools, secondary schools and middle schools. Section 6 defines nursery schools.

- Section 7 imposes a fundamental duty on the parent of every child of compulsory school age to cause their child to receive efficient full-time education suitable to his age, ability and aptitude and to any special educational needs he may have.

- Section 8 defines compulsory school age.

- Section 9 imposes a duty on the secretary of state and local authorities, when exercising or performing all their respective powers and functions under the Education Acts, to have regard to the general principle "that pupils are to be educated in accordance with the wishes of their parents, so far as that is compatible with the provision of efficient instruction and training and the avoidance of unreasonable public expenditure". This duty is particularly relevant in the context of Section I' appeals but it can also be relevant in 'Section F' appeals. It is considered in detail in Chapter 6 of this book.

- Section 19 imposes a duty on a local authority in England to make arrangements for the provision of suitable education at school "or otherwise than at school" for those children of compulsory school age "who, by reason of illness, exclusion from school or otherwise, may not for any period receive suitable education unless such arrangements are made for them" and provides a power in relation to young people.

Section 19 of the 2014 Act imposes a general duty on a local authority in England, when exercising a function under Part 3 in the case of a child or young person, to have regard to certain matters in particular. These are: the views, wishes and feelings of the child and his or her parent, or the young person; the importance of the child and his or her parent, or the young person, participating as fully as possible in decisions relating to the exercise of the function concerned and being provided with the information and support necessary to enable participation in those decisions; the need to support the child and his or her parent, or the young person, in order to facilitate the development of the child or young person and to help him or her achieve the best possible educational and other outcomes. Sections 22 and 23 of the 2014 Act are concerned with identifying children and young people with special educational needs and disabilities.

Chapter 1 of the SEND Code of Practice, entitled 'Principles', addresses sections 19, 22 and 23 of the 2014 Act.

Sections 20 and 21 of the 2014 Act provide the definitions of "special educational needs", "special educational provision", "health care provision" and "social care provision", and are considered further in Chapters 4, 5 and 9 of this book.

Section 24 of the 2014 Act sets out the circumstances in which a local authority is "responsible" for a child or young person for the purposes of Part 3. This issue is considered further in this Chapter, below.

Sections 25, 26 and 28 of the 2014 Act, broadly speaking, are intended to improve the way that services work together to provide support children and young people with educational, health and social care needs. Where these relate to health and social care, they are considered further in Chapter 9 of this book.

Chapter 2 of the Code focuses on the information, advice and support which local authorities must provide for children, young people and parents, in relation to special educational needs, disability, health and social care.

Chapter 3 of the Code explains the duties which local authorities and their partner commissioning bodies have for developing joint arrangements for commissioning services to improve outcomes for children and young people aged 0 to 25 years who have SEN or disabilities.

Chapter 4 of the Code explains the statutory duties on local authorities to develop and publish a 'local offer' setting out the support they expect to be available for local children and young people with SEN or disabilities. These chapters relate to sections 25 to 35 of the 2014 Act. Published information from the 'local offer' may often be relevant evidence in an appeal before the First-tier Tribunal under section 51.

Sections 33 to 35 of the 2014 Act relate to 'mainstream' education. Section 33 is an important provision in the context of section I appeals, by which a child or young person with an EHC plan will be educated in a maintained nursery school, mainstream school or mainstream post-16 institution, unless certain conditions apply. This provision is considered further in Chapter 6, which looks at 'Section I' appeals.

Sections 36-50 of the 2014 Act, regulations 3-31 of the 2014 Regulations and Chapter 9 of the SEND Code of Practice relate to EHC needs assessments and plans including reviews and re-assessments of EHC plans and ceasing to maintain EHC plans. Regulations 17 and 47 contain provisions setting out the circumstances in which an EHC plan or any representations, evidence, advice or information obtained in relation to an EHC plan may be disclosed, the circumstances in which the child or young person's consent to disclosure may be given, and regulation 17(4) provides that the arrangements for keeping a child or young person's EHC plan must be such that they ensure, so far as is reasonably practicable, that unauthorised persons do not have access to it.

Sections 51-60 of the 2014 Act and regulations 32-45 of the 2014 Regulations deal with appeals, mediation and dispute resolution and are supported by Chapter 11 of the Code, entitled 'Resolving Disagreements'. Section 60, however, which relates to claims under the Equality Act 2010, is outside the scope of this book.

Sections 61-65 of the 2014 Act relate to functions of local authorities and sections 66-69 relate to functions of governing bodies and other bodies responsible for the governance of educational institutions such as schools and academies and institutions in the further education sector. Section 61 is an important provision which sets out the circumstances in which a local authority in England may arrange for the special educational provision of a child or young person to be made otherwise than in a school or post-16 institution, by way of home education, for example. Chapter 10 of the SEND Code of Practice, entitled 'Children and young people in specific circumstances' provides statutory guidance in relation children and young people with SEN who are educated at home, in alternative provision, or are in hospital. This is considered in Chapter 7 of this book on appeals for 'EOTAS'.

Section 62 of the 2014 Act enables a local authority in England to make arrangements for a child or young person for whom it maintains an EHC plan to attend an institution outside England and Wales which specialises in providing for children or young people with SEN.

Section 63 of the 2014 Act is an important provision in the context of 'Section I' appeals, whereby a local authority must pay any fees payable in respect of education and training provided by a child or young person at the school, post-16 institution or place at which relevant early years education is provided which is named in the EHC plan of the child or young person which the LA maintains.

Section 66 of the 2014 Act applies in relation to schools and institutions specified in section 66(1), and where a registered pupil or student at such a school or other institution in England has SEN. It imposes a duty on the 'appropriate authorities' of such schools and institutions (e.g. the governing body, in the case of a maintained school) to use their "best endeavours" to secure that the special educational provision called for by the pupil's or student's SEN is made.

Section 69 of the 2014 Act imposes a duty on maintained schools in England and academies to prepare a report containing "SEN information" about the implementation of the governing body's policy for pupils at the school with SEN (and in relation to its duties under the Equality Act 2010 towards pupils and prospective pupils who have disabilities). The "SEN information" report will almost always form a part of the evidence before the First-tier Tribunal in 'Section I' appeals where a maintained school or academy is concerned. Regulations 51, 52 and Schedule 1 of the 2014 Regulations make further provision in relation to "SEN information" reports.

Section 65 of the 2014 Act makes provision for a local authority in England which maintains an EHC plan for a child or young person to access the premises of schools, post-16 institutions and other institutions where education or training is provided in pursuance of the plan, for monitoring purposes.

Sections 70-75 of the 2014 Act relate to detained persons.

Section 76 of the 2014 Act places a duty on the Secretary of State to exercise his or her information-gathering powers to secure SEN information about children and young people under 19 from schools and local authorities and the provision made for them which he thinks would be likely to help in improving the well-being of those children and young people. Section 79 made provision for the Secretary of State and the Lord Chancellor to review and report on how effectively disagreements about the exercise of functions under Part 3 were being resolved; the report was published in 2017.

Sections 77 and 78 of the 2014 Act relate to the SEND Code of Practice. Section 77 specifies the bodies which must have regard to the SEND Code of Practice in the exercise of their functions, and which functions. In 'having regard' to the Code the relevant body must understand it, and, if they decide to depart from it, must explain why, to enable those affected to understand the decision and if necessary, to challenge it: *W v Blaenau Gwent* [2003] EWHC 2880 at [17-18]. If a Tribunal finds guidance in the Code which 'flies in the face' of legislative provisions, it must apply the law as laid down by Parliament – the Code cannot override the statute nor any relevant statutory instrument: *Devon County Council v OH* (SEN) [2016] UKUT 0292 (AAC) at [45]; *Staffordshire County Council v JM* [2016] UKUT 0246 (AAC) at [40].

Section 80 of the 2014 Act is an important provision addressing the situation where parents and young people lack capacity, together with regulations 63-65 and Schedule 3 of the 2014 Regulations and Annex 1 of the SEND Code of Practice. This area is considered in detail in Chapter 10 of this book.

Sitting outside Part 3 but within the 'Education Acts' as listed in section 578(1) of the 1996 Act is section 100 of the 2014 Act ('Duty to support pupils with medical conditions'), which places a duty on the governing body of a maintained school or a pupil referral unit or the proprietor of an Academy school or alternative provision Academy to make arrangements for supporting pupils at the school with medical conditions.

Chapters 5, 6 and 7 of the SEND Code of Practice provide statutory guidance relating to early years providers, schools and further education respectively. Chapter 8, entitled 'Preparing for adulthood from the earliest years' sets out how professionals across education, health and social care should support children and young people with SEN or disabilities to prepare for adult life.

Chapter 10 of the SEND Code of Practice, entitled 'Children and young people in specific circumstances', provides statutory guidance in relation to particular groups of children and young people whose specific circumstances require additional consideration by those who work with them and support their SEN. These groups include looked after children, care leavers, children and young people with SEN and social care needs, including children in need, children and young people who are educated out of area, children and young people with SEN who are educated at home, in alternative provision, or are in hospital, children of service personnel, and children and young people in youth custody.

When is a local authority "responsible" for a child or young person?

By subsection 24(1) of the 2014 Act, a local authority in England is responsible for a child or young person if he or she "is in the authority's area" and has been (a) "identified by the authority as someone who has or may have special educational needs", or (b) "brought to the authority's attention by any person as someone who has or may have special educational needs."

Neither the 2014 Act nor the 2014 Regulations define what is meant by being "in" a local authority's area; nor do they define what it means for a child or young person to "move" from the area of one LA "into the area" of another for the purposes of regulation 13 of the 2014 Regulations, which deals with the transfer of EHC plans from one LA to another.

Similar words were used in section 321(1) of the Education Act 1996 and the Education (Special Educational Needs) (England) (Consolidation) Regulations 2001 SI 2001 No. 3455, regulation 23.

Section 83(6) of the 2014 Act states that a reference in Part 3 to a child or young person who is "in the area" of a local authority in England does not include a child or young person who is wholly or mainly resident in the area of a local authority in Wales or who would be wholly or mainly resident in the area of a local authority in Wales were it not for provision secured for the child or young person under Part 2 of the Additional Learning Needs and Education Tribunal (Wales) Act 2018.

R (JG) v Kent County Council [2016] EWHC 1102 (Admin) was a case under the 1996 Act concerning a family in Kent with a very troubled son who had a statement of special educational needs. The father moved with the son to Sunderland, leaving his wife and their other children in Kent; the family intended that move to be temporary until Kent County Council either arranged for a residential school placement for the child or provided some alternative accommodation in Kent for the father and son. However, Kent County Council decided that the child had "moved" to Sunderland for the purposes of their duties regarding the child. The High Court at [132-134] held that it is necessary to distinguish a situation where there has been a permanent move from one which is temporary or transitory, and it is of assistance to see whether there has been an alteration of a child's ordinary residence to reach a decision as to whether the child has 'moved' for the relevant purpose. Features which have been identified in other contexts for deciding a person's (and especially a child's) ordinary residence may be helpful. However, there are limits on the usefulness of this methodology. The term 'ordinary residence' (or 'habitual residence') was not used in the regulation or the enabling statute, which distinguished the situation in this case from the other authorities cited (for example *R (on the application of Cornwall Council) v Secretary of State for Health* [2015] UKSC 46). A person may have an ordinary residence in more than one place but there can only be one local authority which is responsible for a child's special educational needs. The features identified in the ordinary residence cases are therefore no more than indirect pointers in deciding whether a child "is in the area" of a local authority or has "moved" to the area of another.

Chapter 10 of the 2015 SEND Code of Practice, paragraph 10.8, notes that a significant proportion of looked after children live with foster carers or in a children's home and attend schools in a different local authority area to the local authority that looks after them. Paragraphs 10.8, 10.26 and 10.27 of the Code clearly state that it is the "home" local authority ("where the child normally lives... i.e. ordinarily resident") that is responsible for the child for the purposes of Part 3 of the 2014 Act.

CHAPTER TWO

'REFUSAL TO ASSESS' OR 'RE-ASSESS' APPEALS

Section 51 of the Children and Families Act 2014 Part 3 affords a right to a child's parent or a young person (subject to mediation) to appeal to the First-tier Tribunal against a decision of a local authority not to secure an EHC needs assessment for the child or young person (section 51(2)(a)) or not to secure a re-assessment of the needs of the child or young person under section 44 following a request to do so (section 51(2)(d)).

The key provisions under the 2014 act relating to EHC needs assessments and re-assessments are section 36 (EHC needs assessments) and 44 (re-assessments). The key provisions under the Special Educational Needs and Disability Regulations 2014 are regulations 3 to 10 and 24 to 27. Paragraphs 9.8 to 5.52 of the SEND Code of Practice deal with EHC needs assessments and paragraphs 9.186 to 9.192 deal with re-assessments.

EHC needs assessments

An "EHC needs assessment" is an assessment of the educational, health care and social care needs of a child or young person: subsection 36(2) of the 2014 Act.

Regulation 6 of the 2014 Regulations sets out the information and advice to be obtained in EHC Needs Assessments. The local authority must gather advice and information from the child's parent or the young person and from relevant professionals about the child or young person's education, health and care needs, desired outcomes, and provision that may be required. The types of advice and information that the LA must seek for the assessment comprises: (a) advice and information from the child's parent or the young person; (b) educational advice and information from the head teacher or principal of the school or post-16 or other institution that the child or young person is attending (where this is not available, the LA must seek advice from a person with experience of teaching children or young people with SEN or knowledge of the provision which may be called for to meet those needs; if such advice is not available, and if the child or young person is not currently attending a school or post-16 or other institution, the LA must seek advice from a person responsible for educational provision for the child or young person); if any parent of the child or young person is a serving member of Her Majesty's armed forces, also from the Secretary of State for Defence; (c) medical advice and information from a health care professional identified by the responsible commissioning body; (d) psychological advice and information from an educational psychologist; (e) advice and information in relation to social care; (f) advice and information from any other person the LA thinks is appropriate; (g) where the child or young person is in or beyond year 9, advice and information in relation to provision to assist the child or young person in preparation for adulthood and independent living; and (h) advice and information from any person the child's parent or young person reasonably requests that the LA seek advice from. If the child or young person in question is either hearing or visually impaired, or both, the educational advice and information must be given after consultation with a person who is qualified to teach children or young people with these impairments.

The SEND Code of Practice, at paragraphs 9.32 to 9.34, stresses that local authorities and their partners should establish local protocols for the effective sharing of information which addresses confidentiality, consent and security of information. As far as possible there should be a 'tell us once' approach to sharing information during the assessment so that families and young people do not have to repeat the same information to different agencies or different practitioners and services within each agency. However, LAs must discuss with the child and young person what information they are happy for the LA to share with other agencies, and a record should be made of what information can be shared and with whom.

A request for a local authority in England to secure an EHC needs assessment for a child or young person may be made to the LA by the child's parent, the young person or a person acting on behalf of a school or post-16 institution: subsection 36(1).

When a request under subsection 36(1) is made to a local authority, or a LA otherwise becomes responsible for a child or young person, the LA must determine "whether it may be necessary for special educational provision to be made for the child or young person in accordance with an EHC plan": subsection 36(3). By subsection 36(4), in making a determination under section 36(3), the LA must consult the child's parent or the young person. Subsection 36(10) provides that, in making a determination or forming an opinion for the purposes of section 36 in relation to a young person aged over 18, a local authority must consider whether he or she requires additional time, in comparison to the majority of others of the same age who do not have special educational needs, to complete his or her education or training.

Where the local authority determines that it is not necessary for special educational provision to be made for the child or young person in accordance with an EHC plan, it must notify the child's parent or the young person: (a) of the reasons for that determination, and (b) that accordingly it has decided not to secure an EHC needs assessment for the child or young person: subsection 36(5).

It follows that a 'refusal to assess' appeal under subsection 51(2)(a) will arise where a local authority has determined that it is not necessary for special educational provision to be made for the child or young person in accordance with an EHC plan and has given notification in accordance with subsection 36(5). However, subsections 36(6) and 36(7) make provision for circumstances where no request has been made but the LA determines that it may be necessary for special educational provision to be made for the child or young person in accordance with an EHC plan. In the prescribed circumstances, the LA must notify the parent or young person of their right to express views and submit evidence to the authority. Subsection 36(8) requires the LA to secure an EHC needs assessment for the child or young person if, after having regard to any views expressed and evidence submitted under section 36(7), the LA is of the opinion that the child or young person has or may have special educational needs, and it may be necessary for special educational provision to be made for the child or young person in accordance with an EHC plan.

The relevant regulations are regulations 3 to 10 of the Special Educational Needs and Disability Regulations 2014.

Regulation 3 requires the local authority to consult the child's parent or the young person as soon as practicable after receiving a request for an EHC needs assessment under section 36(1) of the Act, before determining whether it may be necessary for special educational provision to be made in accordance with an EHC plan for the child or young person.

By regulation 4(1) and regulation 5(1), where a local authority determines that it is <u>not</u> necessary for special educational provision to be made in accordance with an EHC plan it must notify the child's parent or the young person in accordance with section 36(5) of the Act as soon as practicable, but in any event within 6 weeks of receiving a request for an EHC needs assessment under section 36(1) of the Act or becoming responsible for the child or young person in accordance with section 24 of the Act. It must also notify them of their right to appeal that decision, the time limits for doing so, the information concerning mediation, set out in regulation 32, and the availability of disagreement resolution services and information and advice about matters relating to the special educational needs of children and young people. However, the LA need not comply with the time limit referred to in regulation 5(1) if it is impractical to do so because of any of the situations specified in regulation 5(4) apply.

In *Cambridgeshire County Council v FL-J* [2016] UKUT 225 (AAC) the First-tier tribunal decided that the local authority <u>should</u> secure an assessment. In the Upper Tribunal, Jacobs J rejected the LA's ground of appeal against that decision which related to the issue of necessity. Jacobs J held, at [11], that the First-tier Tribunal, hearing an appeal against a decision not to secure an assessment, had to make a provisional predictive judgment about the likely need for special educational provision; it did not have to make a definitive decision. The factual issues that were argued out by the parties in their response and reply on the appeal might well be relevant to, if not determinative of, the final decision under *section 37*, but that was not within the Tribunal's jurisdiction to decide in an appeal under section 51(2)(a). In an appeal under section 51(2)(a), the Tribunal only had to decide whether the threshold questions for the making of an assessment were satisfied, and that did not need to be done with so great a degree of certainty. Its findings and reasons were entitled at that initial stage to reflect the degree of uncertainty that is inherently likely before an assessment is actually made. Jacobs J held, at [4], that when the authority or the tribunal is deciding whether an assessment should be secured, two different questions arise. One is a question of present fact: 'has' the young person a learning difficulty or disability? The other is a prediction: is it one that 'calls for' special educational provision (section 20(1)) or for which such provision 'may be necessary' (section 36(3))? Those different expressions are both framed according to the stage of the process. The LA or tribunal does not have to decide at this initial stage whether special educational provision 'is necessary' (section 37(1)); that question only arises when an assessment has been made. The issue at the initial stage is a provisional and predictive one; it is only when an assessment has been made that a definitive decision has to be made.

In *RB v Calderdale MBC* (SEN) [2018] UKUT 390 (AAC) the First-tier tribunal decided <u>not</u> to uphold the parent's appeal against the local authority's decision not to secure an assessment in respect of her child. R was an able student, but had a diagnosis of indeterminate colitis, one consequence of which was that he had missed a significant amount of schooling. The LA argued that R's needs could be supported at school by a health care plan. The First-tier Tribunal accepted that R's illness was a disability which prevented and hindered him from making use of facilities of a kind generally provided in mainstream schools for the purposes of section 20(2)(b) of the 2014 Act (which defines special educational needs), 'in the sense that he is not able to attend school at present', but it did not consider that it fell within the definition of section 20(1) because it did not call for special educational provision to be made for him (defined in section 21(1) as educational or training provision that is additional to, or different from, that made generally for others of the same age in mainstream schools in England). The First-tier Tribunal found that the provision the parent regarded as necessary – which included a laptop for any time that he was too ill to attend school, home tuition and counselling – was no different to the provision generally available to other children at mainstream school. The Upper Tribunal (Wikeley J) held, at [21-22], that the First-tier Tribunal had focused, incorrectly, on the fact that R did not have a learning difficulty and did not require curriculum differentiation. It had failed to give sufficient weight to the fact that R was not at school at the material time and had failed to consider what provision *might* be necessary to ensure that he was able to return to school. It had missed the point that interventions to enable him to return to (and remain at) school, such as home tuition and help to address the mental health issues associated with his physical disability, *might* have fallen within the definition of special educational provision. It had lost sight of the question it had to answer under section 36(3), namely "whether it may be necessary for special educational provision to be made for the child or young person in accordance with an EHC plan."

Under section 323 of the Education Act 1996, the statutory test for assessment was: (a) does the child have special educational needs, and (b) is it necessary for the authority to determine the special educational provision which any learning difficulty he may have calls for? In *Buckinghamshire County Council v HW (SEN)* [2013] UKUT 0470 (AAC) at [7] Jacobs J considered it thus: there were two conditions in subsection 323(2): one was a matter of fact: did the child have special educational needs? The other was a matter of judgment: was it necessary to determine the special educational provision that any learning difficulties she might have called for? As for the meaning of the word, 'necessary', Jacobs J stated, at [16]: "There may well be sufficient flexibility in the meaning of *necessary* to avoid any such discussion. Although in the dictionary this word is defined in terms of what is essential or indispensable, in practice it is used less strictly. That meaning is captured by the European Court of Human Rights in *The Sunday Times v United Kingdom* (1979) 2 EHRR 245 at [59]. The Court said that it was neither synonymous with *indispensable* nor equivalent to *useful*, *reasonable* or *desirable*. Rather it connoted a *pressing social need*. That would not be an appropriate test in the context of the Education Act, which is significantly different from the European Convention on Human Rights. But the point remains valid. *Necessary* sets a standard that is somewhere between *indispensable* and *useful* or *reasonable*. I am not going to define it more precisely. It is a word in general usage and it is that usage that the tribunal must apply."

In *The Royal Borough of Kensington & Chelsea v* GG (SEN) [2017] UKUT 0141 (AAC) the Upper Tribunal held, at [80-82], that if the provision sought by the young person in question was higher education, that would not be a form of special educational provision for the purposes of Part 3 of the 2014 Act given the exclusion of HE from the definition of "education" by section 83(4). An assessment would therefore be pointless because it could not lead to an EHC plan that would deliver what the young person wants. However, a vague aspiration to pursue HE or the inclusion of HE amongst the educational options that a young person is thinking of pursuing should not be seized upon as a reason to exclude them from the system of entitlements under Part 3 of the 2014 Act. In this respect, local authorities should bear in mind their general obligations under sections 19 and 32 of the 2014 Act: they may need to explain to a young person that, if he wishes to pursue HE, Part 3 of the 2014 Act cannot operate to support him through a course of HE. Also, a course is not necessarily a HE course because it is provided by, or under arrangement with, an institution within the HE sector. What matters is whether the course falls within the list specified in Schedule 6 to Education Reform Act 1998.

The SEND Code of Practice addresses EHC needs assessments at paragraphs 9.8-9.19 of Chapter 9.

Paragraph 9.14 states that, in considering whether an EHC needs assessment is necessary, the local authority should consider whether there is evidence that despite the early years provider, school or post-16 institution having taken relevant and purposeful action to identify, assess and meet the special educational needs of the child or young person, the child or young person has not made expected progress. To inform their decision the LA will need to take into account a wide range of evidence, and should pay particular attention to: evidence of the child or young person's academic attainment (or developmental milestones in younger children) and rate of progress; information about the nature, extent and context of the child or young person's SEN, evidence of action already being taken by the early years provider, school or post-16 institution to meet the child or young person's SEN; evidence that where progress has been made, it has only been as the result of much additional intervention and support over and above that which is usually provided; evidence of the child or young person's physical, emotional and social development and health needs, drawing on relevant evidence from clinicians and other health professionals and what has been done to meet these by other agencies.

Paragraph 9.15 adds that a young person who was well supported through the Local Offer whilst at school may move to a further education (FE) college where the same range or level of support is not available and an EHC plan may then be needed. It also may be the case that young people acquire SEN through illness or accident or have a condition that requires increasing support as they get older.

Paragraph 9.16 points out that local authorities may develop criteria as guidelines to help them decide when it is necessary to carry out an EHC needs assessment, but they must not apply a 'blanket' policy as this would prevent the consideration of a child's or young person's needs individually and on their merits.

Re-assessments

Section 44 of the 2014 Act and regulations 23 to 28 make provision for re-assessment of EHC needs.

By subsection 44(2) a local authority must secure a re-assessment of the educational, health care and social care needs of a child or young person for whom it maintains an EHC plan if a request is made to it by (a) the child's parent or the young person, or (b) the governing body, proprietor or principal of the school, post-16 institution or other institution which the child or young person attends. However, this is subject to regulations made under subsection 44(7)(b), and by regulation 24 of the 2014 regulations, the LA does not need to do so where it has carried out an assessment or re-assessment within the period of six months prior to that request or it is "not necessary" for the LA to make a further assessment.

By subsection 44(5), in deciding whether to secure a re-assessment of the needs of a young person aged over 18 for whom an EHC plan is maintained, a local authority must have regard to whether the educational or training outcomes specified in the plan have been achieved.

By regulation 25(1), the local authority must notify the child's parent or the young person whether or not it is necessary to re-assess the child or young person within 15 days of receiving the request to re-assess. By regulation 25(2), where the LA does not need to re-assess the child or young person the notification under regulation 25(1) must also notify the child's parent or the young person of their right to appeal matters within the EHC plan in accordance with section 51(2)(d) of the Act, the time limits for doing so, the information concerning mediation, set out in regulation 32; and the availability of disagreement resolution services and advice and information about matters relating to the special educational needs of children and young people.

Powers of the First-tier Tribunal in 'refusal to assess' or 're-assess' appeals, and compliance

By regulation 43(2)(a) and (b) of the 2014 Regulations, when determining an appeal made under section 51(2)(a) or (d), the powers of the First-tier Tribunal include the power to dismiss the appeal or to order the local authority to arrange an assessment of the child or young person under section 36 or a re-assessment under section 44(2) where the LA has refused to do so.

By regulation 44(2)(b), where the order of the First-tier Tribunal requires a local authority to make an assessment or re-assessment, the LA shall within 2 weeks of the order being made notify the child's parent or the young person that it shall make the assessment or re-assessment. Where, following the assessment or re-assessment, the LA decides that it is not necessary for special educational provision to be made for the child or the young person, in accordance with an EHC plan, the LA shall notify the child's parent or the young person of its decision, giving reasons for it as soon as practicable, and in any event within 10 weeks of the date of the First-tier Tribunal's order. Where, following the assessment or re-assessment, the LA decides that it is necessary for special educational provision to be made for the child or the young person, in accordance with an EHC plan, it must send the finalised plan to the child's parent or young person under regulation 14(3) and to those specified in regulation 13(2) as soon as practicable and in any event within 14 weeks of the date of the First-tier Tribunal's order. Regulation 44(2) is subject any direction made by the First-tier Tribunal: regulation 44(1).

In an unopposed appeal, the Tribunal is not required to make an order. By regulation 45(3), the local authority must, within 2 weeks of the date it notifies the First-tier Tribunal that it will not oppose the appeal before it submits a response, notify the child's parent or the young person that it must make the EHC needs assessment or re-assessment. If, following the EHC needs assessment or re-assessment, the LA decides that it is not necessary to make and maintain an EHC plan, it must notify the child's parent or the young person of its decision, giving reasons for it as soon as practicable, and in any event within 10 weeks of the date it notified the First-tier Tribunal that it would not oppose the appeal: regulation 45(3A)(a). If the LA decides that it is necessary to make an EHC plan, it must send the finalised plan to the child's parent or the young person under regulation 14(2) and those specified in regulation 13(2) as soon as practicable and in any event within 14 weeks of the date it notified the First-tier Tribunal that it would not oppose the appeal: regulation 45(3A)(b).

However, by regulation 44(3) and 45(7) the local authority need not comply with the above time limits if it is impractical to do so because (a) exceptional personal circumstances affect the child or their parent, or the young person during that period of time; (b) the child or their parent or the young person is absent from the area of the LA for a continuous period of 2 weeks or more during that period of time; or (c) any of the circumstances referred to in regulation 13(3) apply.

The circumstances referred to in regulation 13(3) are if it is impractical for any of the reasons set out in regulation 10(4)(a) to (d). Those reasons are: (a) the local authority has requested advice from the head teacher or principal of a school or post-16 institution during a period beginning one week before any date on which that school or institution was closed for a continuous period of not less than 4 weeks from that date and ending one week before the date on which it re-opens; (b) the LA has requested advice from the person identified as having responsibility for special educational needs (if any) in relation to, or other person responsible for, a child's education at a provider of relevant early years education during a period beginning one week before any date on which that provider was closed for a continuous period of not less than 4 weeks from that date and ending one week before the date on which it re-opens; (c) exceptional personal circumstances affect the child or the child's parent, or the young person during that time period; or (d) the child or the child's parent, or the young person, are absent from the area of the authority for a continuous period of not less than 4 weeks during that time period.

CHAPTER THREE

'REFUSAL TO ISSUE' APPEALS

Section 51 of the Children and Families Act 2014 Part 3 affords a right to a child's parent or a young person (subject to mediation) to appeal to the First-tier Tribunal against a decision of a local authority, following an EHC needs assessment, that it is not necessary for special educational provision to be made for the child or young person in accordance with an EHC plan: section 51(2)(b) of the 2014 Act – a decision not to make and maintain an EHC plan.

The key provisions under the 2014 Act relating to 'refusal to issue' appeals are sections 36 and 37.

Section 37(1) provides: "Where, in the light of an EHC needs assessment, it is necessary for special educational provision to be made for a child or young person in accordance with an EHC plan— (a) the local authority must secure that an EHC plan is prepared for the child or young person, and (b) once an EHC plan has been prepared, it must maintain the plan."

By section 36(9), after an EHC needs assessment has been carried out, the local authority must notify the child's parent or the young person of the outcome of the assessment, whether it proposes to secure that an EHC plan is prepared for the child or young person, and the reasons for that decision.

The SEND Code of Practice, at paragraphs 9.54 to 9.56, gives statutory guidance on the decision whether to make special educational provision in accordance with an EHC plan.

By regulation 10, where the local authority decides that it is not necessary for special educational provision to be made for a child or young person in accordance with an EHC plan, the notification given in accordance with section 36(9) must be given as soon as practicable, and in any event within 16 weeks of the LA receiving a request for an EHC needs assessment in accordance with section 36(1) of the Act, or of the LA becoming responsible for the child or young person in accordance with section 24 of the Act.

The statutory test at section 37(1) has given rise to a substantial amount of case law.

Nottinghamshire County Council v SF and GD [2020] EWCA Civ 226 was the first time that the Court of Appeal had to consider the meaning of "necessary" in section 37 of the 2014 Act or for that matter the equivalent provision in the Education Act 1996.

The Court of Appeal, at [8-10], noted the context and legal framework: by section 66 of the 2014 Act, children who do not have an EHC plan are owed a statutory duty by the governing body of their school to use its "best endeavours" to secure the special educational provision that they need. This duty is not absolute so that resource constraints may be taken into account. By contrast, children with an EHC plan are owed an absolute duty by the local authority to make the provision specified in the EHC plan. Resource constraints are irrelevant once special educational provision has been identified in the EHC plan. By section 37(1) of the 2014 Act, an EHC plan will only be made for a child if it is necessary for special educational provision to be made in accordance with an EHC plan. A decision not to make an EHC plan can be appealed to the First-tier Tribunal but the Tribunal has no jurisdiction in relation to section 66 arrangements.

At [20-27], the Court Appeal the reviewed Upper Tribunal's case law, summarising and agreeing with it thus, at [20]: "The essence of the UT's case law is that what is necessary is an evaluative judgment based upon the specific facts of the particular case which are for the specialist tribunal to deduce from the evidence in each case. It is not a concept that is to be over-defined."

In *Buckinghamshire CC v HW* [2013] ELR 519 Jacobs J held that 'necessary' (under the Education Act 1996) has a spectrum of meanings, "somewhere between indispensable and useful". He emphasised that it was a word in common usage, and it is that which a tribunal must apply.

In *Manchester City Council v JW* [2014] UKUT 168, Mark J noted at [14] that what is 'necessary' may involve a value judgment.

In *Hertfordshire CC v MC and KC* (SEN) [2016] UKUT 0385 (AAC) Lane J cited both of the above decisions with approval before adding, at [36], that "what is 'necessary' is a matter to be deduced rather than defined. Its determination will vary according to the circumstances of a particular case and may well involve a considerable degree of judgment". Lane J also considered the effect of the Code of Practice in *Hertfordshire*. At [27] she noted that "the Code envisages that the majority of children with additional educational needs will not require EHC Plans. Their needs will be met in a mainstream setting from resources normally available at mainstream schools." She considered paragraphs 9.53 to 9.55 of the Code before summarising a paradigm case in the following way (at [29]): "(a) What did we know before? [the assessment] (b) What do we know now? [after the assessment] (c) If (a) and (b) are well matched, an EHC Plan is probably not necessary; but (d) If the child is not making progress/sufficient progress despite (a) and (b) being well matched, can appropriate provision be made from normal mainstream resources? Or may the Local Authority have to go further and issue a plan? In other words, which side of the line does the case fall on." And then finally: "Point (d) is no more than a restatement of the question 'is an EHC Plan necessary?'"

Lane J also cited Judge Mark in *Manchester* at [32] as follows: "I bear in mind that the Code of Practice is precisely what it is said to be – guidance to which the local authority and tribunal must have regard. It does not affect the generality of section 324 [under the Education Act 1996] so as to exclude any possibility that a statement may be necessary for some other reason than those indicated in the guidance". Lane J also held at [19]: "The Code is not, however, binding law. Where there is a difference between the law as set out in statutes, regulations and case law, and the Code, the Tribunal must follow the law".

This summary of the Upper Tribunal's case law did not include *NC & DH v Leicestershire CC* [2012] UKUT 85 (AAC) *SC and MS v Worcestershire CC (SEN) [2016] UKUT 267 (AAC).*

In *NC & DH v Leicestershire CC* [2012] UKUT 85 (AAC) HHJ Pearl held, at [32], that two questions must be addressed in applying section 324 (that is deciding whether a local authority is required to make and maintain a statement): "The first question is whether the special educational provision identified as necessary for the child in the assessment carried out under section 323 is in fact available within the resources normally available to a mainstream school... The second question is, if so, can the school reasonably be expected to make such provision from within its resources".

In *SC and MS v Worcestershire CC (SEN)* [2016] UKUT 267 *(AAC)* Mitchell J stated at [40]:

> "The question whether it is "necessary" to determine special educational provision has to informed by the wider legislative scheme of which the statementing provisions are part. If a statement is made, the child enters a world of specific educational entitlements that are not enjoyed by other children. In particular:
>
> (a) the local authority must "arrange that the special educational provision specified in the statement is made for the child" (section 324(5)(a)). The specification of a school in a statement involves specifying special educational provision, as is made clear by sections 324(3) & (4). Section 324(3) requires the statement to specify the special educational provision needed "including the particulars required by subsection (4)". Within those particulars, we find "the name of any school or institution...which they consider would be appropriate for the child and should be specified

in the statement" (this does not apply if the parent's preferred maintained school is already required to be specified by Schedule 27 to EA 1996). If the specified school is an independent school, section 324(5)(a) requires the authority to fund the child's education at the school but, if there were any doubt about this, section 348(2) puts it beyond doubt;

(b) if the name of a maintained school is specified in the statement, the school's governing body must admit the child to the school. This even overrides the statutory class size limit in section 1 of the School Standards and Framework Act 1998;

(c) statements are entrenched to a significant degree because Schedule 27(2A) to the EA 1996 only permits an amendment in three cases: following a statutory review carried out in accordance with the procedure laid down in Schedule 27; where ordered by the tribunal; where directed by the Secretary of State;

(d) if a child moves to the area of a different local authority, his/her statement is transferred. The new authority is required to arrange the special educational provision specified in the statement (regulation 23 of the 2000 Regulations). Hence, the new authority cannot immediately argue that, because it is less well-resourced than the previous authority, the educational provision specified imposes an unreasonable burden. The provision specified may only be amended in accordance with the statutory procedures for altering statements;

(e) a local authority does not have a free hand to cease to maintain a statement. The test is whether "it is no longer necessary to maintain it" (Schedule 27(11)(1) to EA 1996). And provision is made so that a determination not to maintain cannot take effect until any appeal is determined or withdrawn (Schedule 27(11)(5));

(f) statements must be regularly reviewed, at least annually, with the review taking the form of a re-assessment (section 328(1))."

These specific educational entitlements continue to apply under the 2014 Act in relation to EHC plans. By section 42(2) the responsible local authority must secure the specified special educational provision for the child or young person. Section 43 requires any maintained school or maintained nursery school in England, Academy, institution within the further education sector in England, non-maintained special school England or institution approved by the Secretary of State under section 41 to admit the child or young person for whom the EHC plan is maintained if that school or institution is named in Section I of the plan. Regulation 15 of the 2014 Regulations makes provision for the transfer of EHC plans. Section 45 and regulations 29 to 31 prescribe the circumstances in which a LA may cease to maintain a plan, and the procedure for doing so. Section 44 and regulations 22 to 28 of the 2014 Regulations set out the circumstances in which the plan must be reviewed (or needs re-assessed), the circumstances in which the content of the plan may be amended, and the procedures for doing so.

At [41-43] of *SC and MS v Worcestershire CC* Mitchell J further stated:

> "41. A statement therefore generates certainty of, and a significant degree of stability in, educational provision. The child is insulated in part from the trade-offs that, for other children, are an inevitable part of fixing their state educational provision. And so the legislative scheme shows that, for certain children with learning difficulties, Parliament decided not to rely on general statutory education obligations, including a governing body's section 317(1) "best endeavours" duty, to secure an appropriate education for the child. For certain children, an additional guarantee of appropriate educational provision was created. This should be taken into account in deciding whether it is necessary to determine a child's special educational provision.
>
> 42. If there is a realistic doubt that the operation of the "best endeavours" duty, and other relevant statutory duties, would result in the required provision, that favours a conclusion that the duty to make and maintain a statement arises because it is a case where it is "necessary" to determine special educational provision

> (in *Buckinghamshire CC v HW* [2013] ELR 519, Upper Tribunal Judge Jacobs described necessity as falling somewhere between indispensable and useful, but that he was not going to define more precisely).
>
> 43. That doubt may arise for a number of reasons. For example, the child's history of educational provision may lead a decision maker to conclude that, without a statement, the required provision is unlikely to materialise. This reflects what Judge Mark said in *Manchester City Council v JW* [2014] UKUT 0168 (AAC): "if it was the case that a school or local authority, despite having the necessary resources, simply refused to use their best endeavours to provide the requisite special educational provision, a tribunal may well consider it necessary to direct a statement". And the nature of the special educational provision in question may, of itself, due to its quantity, specialist nature or for other reasons, lead to the conclusion that a statement is needed in order to ensure appropriate provision is made."

At [49] Mitchell J further stated, in relation to the statement of HHJ Pearl in *NC & DH v Leicestershire CC* [2012] UKUT 85 (AAC) at [32], "While I do not disagree, I think perhaps a more practical route to the same destination is simply to ask whether, without a statement, the decision maker can be satisfied, to a reasonable degree of certainty, that the required educational provision will be delivered. In answering that question, regard should be had to the legal consequences of a statement as described in paragraph 40 above."

This formulation is sometimes summarised as the 'can/will test'.

In *CB v Birmingham CC* [2018] UKUT 13 (AAC) Lane J stated at [16]-[17]:

> "16. In my view, there is a clear, albeit rough and ready resource line to be crossed before an EHC plan is considered to be necessary. It is based on the kinds of provision a school could make from its own notional SEN budget.

> 17. It is also plain, in my view, that the provision the LA expects to make available as published in its local offer is a relevant consideration in working out what will, on balance, be available from a school's internal resources. It is open to a parent who disbelieves the local offer to provide evidence showing that it does not represent what is expected to be available, or that a particular school will not be able to make the provision expected under the local offer. Neither may be easy for a parent to establish, not least because of the SEN budget available to each school. Of course, if such evidence were adduced, a tribunal would have to decide its weight."

However, it is clear from the above authorities, in particular *Nottinghamshire CC v SF and GD*, that if the relevant resource line is not or would not be crossed, that is not necessarily determinative.

It is also clear, from *Nottinghamshire CC v SF and GD* at [39], that the question requires a consideration of the provision which is additional to or different from that made generally for others of the same age in mainstream schools *in England*, not within the local authority's own area, as was the case under the 1996 Act. That is the effect of section 21(1) of the 2014 Act.

As stated in paragraph 9.6 of the Code of Practice, an EHC needs assessment will not always lead to an EHC plan. The information gathered during an EHC needs assessment may indicate ways in which the school, college or other provider can meet the child or young person's needs without an EHC plan.

Powers of the First-tier Tribunal in 'refusal to issue' appeals, and compliance

By regulation 43(2)(a), (c) and (d), the powers of the First-tier Tribunal include the power to dismiss the appeal, or to order the local authority to make and maintain an EHC Plan where the LA has refused to do so (reg. 43(2)(c)), or to refer the case back to the LA for them to reconsider whether, having regard to any observations made by the First-tier Tribunal, it is necessary for the LA to determine the special educational provision for the child or young person (reg. 43(2)(d)).

By regulation 44(2)(d), where the order refers the case back to the local authority for it to reconsider, the LA shall do so within 2 weeks of the order being made and shall either send a copy of the draft EHC Plan as required under Regulation 13 or give notice as required under Regulation 5 of any decision not to maintain an EHC Plan.

By regulation 44(2)(c), where the order requires the local authority to make and maintain an EHC Plan, the LA shall issue a draft EHC Plan within 5 weeks of the order being made; and send a copy of the finalised EHC plan to the child's parent or young person under regulation 14(2) and to those specified in regulation 13(2), within 11 weeks of the order being made.

Regulation 44(2) is subject any direction made by the First-tier Tribunal: regulation 44(1).

In an unopposed appeal, the Tribunal is not required to make an order. By regulation 45(6), where the appeal is made under section 51(2)(b) of the 2014 Act, the local authority must issue a draft EHC plan within 5 weeks of the date it notifies the First-tier Tribunal that it will not oppose the appeal before it submits a response, and send a copy of the finalised EHC plan to the child's parent or the young person under regulation 14(2) and to those specified in regulation 13(2), within 11 weeks of the date it notified the First-tier Tribunal that it would not oppose the appeal.

However, by regulation 44(3) and 45(7), the local authority need not comply with the time limits set out in regulations 44(2)(c) and 45(6) if it is impractical to do so because (a) exceptional personal circumstances affect the child or their parent, or the young person during that period of time; (b) the child or their parent or the young person is absent from the area of the authority for a continuous period of 2 weeks or more during that period of time; or (c) any of the circumstances referred to in regulation 13(3) apply.

The circumstances referred to in regulation 13(3) are if it is impractical for any of the reasons set out in regulation 10(4)(a) to (d). Those reasons are: (a) the local authority has requested advice from the head teacher or principal of a school or post-16 institution during a period beginning one week before any date on which that school or institution was closed for a continuous period of not less than 4 weeks from that date and ending one week before the date on which it re-opens; (b) the LA has requested advice from the person identified as having responsibility for special educational needs (if any) in relation to, or other person responsible for, a child's education at a provider of relevant early years education during a period beginning one week before any date on which that provider was closed for a continuous period of not less than 4 weeks from that date and ending one week before the date on which it re-opens; (c) exceptional personal circumstances affect the child or the child's parent, or the young person during that time period; or (d) the child or the child's parent, or the young person, are absent from the area of the authority for a continuous period of not less than 4 weeks during that time period.

CHAPTER FOUR

SPECIAL EDUCATIONAL NEEDS AND 'SECTION B' APPEALS

Sections 20 and 21 of the Children and Families Act 2014 Part 3, which define special educational needs and special education provision, and regulation 12(1)(b) of the Special Educational Needs and Disability Regulations 2014, are the key provisions which govern Section B of EHC plans. Regulation 12(1)(b) requires the child or young person's special educational needs to be set out in Section B of the EHC plan.

Subsections 51(1), (2)(c)(i) and (e) of the 2014 Act make provision for 'Section B' appeals. A child's parent or a young person may appeal to the First-tier Tribunal against the matters set out in subsection 51(2), subject to section 55 (mediation). Subsection 51(2)(c)(i) sets out: where an EHC plan is maintained for the child or young person, the child's or young person's special educational needs as specified in the plan. Subsection 51(2)(e) sets out: a decision of a local authority not to secure the amendment or replacement of an EHC plan it maintains for the child or young person following a review or re-assessment under section 44. By subsection 51(3), the circumstances in which a parent or young person may bring an appeal under subsection 51(2(c) are when an EHC plan is first finalised (s. 51(3)(a)) and following an amendment or replacement of the plan (s. 51(3)(b)).

Regulations 18 to 28 of the 2014 Regulations deal with reviewing, re-assessing, amending and replacing EHC plans.

Section 20 of the 2014 Act defines "special educational needs" for the purposes of Part 3 and states:

20 When a child or young person has special educational needs

(1) A child or young person has special educational needs if he or she has a learning difficulty or disability which calls for special educational provision to be made for him or her.

(2) A child of compulsory school age or a young person has a learning difficulty or disability if he or she—

(a) has a significantly greater difficulty in learning than the majority of others of the same age, or

(b) has a disability which prevents or hinders him or her from making use of facilities of a kind generally provided for others of the same age in mainstream schools or mainstream post-16 institutions.

(3) A child under compulsory school age has a learning difficulty or disability if he or she is likely to be within subsection (2) when of compulsory school age (or would be likely, if no special educational provision were made).

(4) A child or young person does not have a learning difficulty or disability solely because the language (or form of language) in which he or she is or will be taught is different from a language (or form of language) which is or has been spoken at home.

(5) This section applies for the purposes of this Part.

It may be seen from the above that the statutory definition of special educational *needs* is closely connected with the concept of special educational *provision*, which is defined by section 21 of the 2014 Act. A child or young person may have a learning difficulty or disability (as defined) but he or she will *not* have special educational needs ('SEN') *unless* that learning difficulty or disability 'calls for' special educational provision to be made for him or her. Because the definition of 'special educational provision' includes health or social care provision which 'educates or trains' the young person, learning difficulties or disabilities which 'call for' such provision will also be SEN. The law in relation to the definition of 'special educational provision' is explained further in Chapter 5.

Consideration of a child's or young person's SEN will involve a consideration of whether special educational provision is *called for* but should *not* involve a decision in relation to *what* special educational provision is required to meet those needs. The content of Section B should *not* be decided with reference to Section F. In *A v SENT & Barnet LBC* [2003] EWHC 3368 at [17] the High Court (Lloyd Jones QC) stated: "it is the duty of a local education authority to decide first what are a child's special educational needs within Part 2, secondly what special educational provision is necessary to meet those needs within Part 3… These questions have to be addressed in this order because it is only when a decision has been taken as to a child's special educational needs that it is possible to decide what provision is required to meet them." In *The Learning Trust v MP* [2007] EWHC 1634 (Admin), [2007] ELR 658 the High Court (Nicol QC) observed at [40], that Parts 2 and 3 of a statement have been likened to a medical diagnosis and prescription (R *v Secretary of State for Education and Science ex parte E* [1992] 1 FLR 377, 388-389), and stated, "It is important then to identify or diagnose the need before going on to prescribe the educational provision to which that need gives rise…"

H v A London Borough (SEN) [2015] UKUT 0316 (AAC) was a case in which the First-tier Tribunal's thinking in relation to the child's learning difficulty, behaviours, and the special educational provision called for by his learning difficulty, became confused. The appeal concerned a child with Asperger's Syndrome and a history of significant mental health difficulties who engaged in sexually harmful behaviours. The First-tier Tribunal acknowledged that the child was on the autistic spectrum and had social communication needs but did not accept that his sexualised behaviour was inherent as or a manifestation of a special need: it considered that this behaviour was 'learned' at a residential school where, it was said, older pupils spent long hours unsupervised watching pornographic material, and at a subsequent school, when he was the victim of some form of sexual bullying or abuse. Ward J, at [28b], accepted that the First-tier Tribunal was entitled to find that the child's sexually harmful behaviour was not part of his learning difficulty. However, the question was what properly flowed from what the Tribunal *did* find to be his learning difficulty.

It is not the case that Section B may *only* contain a description of the child's or young person's special educational needs. In the case of *W v Leeds County Council* [2002] EWCA Civ 988 it was argued on behalf of the appellant parent that because Part 2 of the child's statement spoke of his need for "constant supervision" whereas in Part 3 provision was made for "constant adult supervision during school hours" the statement was unlawful because the need identified in Part 2 was not limited to "school hours". The Court of Appeal was referred to the case of *R v Secretary of State for Education and Science ex parte E* [1992] 1 FLR 377 (in which Part 2 of the child's statement had identified a difficulty but Part 3 had failed to make appropriate provision to meet it) and concluded, at [35]: "…it does not follow from the decision in *Ex parte E*, that every word or phrase used in Part 2 is deemed to represent, or must indeed constitute an educational need. Neither the Act nor the Regulations require that Part 2 should omit reference to matters which represent narrative account, background or context to the special educational needs of the child, and indeed it would be very surprising if it were to do so, not least because there may well be ongoing learning difficulties requiring reassessment by way of review. Although Part 2 must identify the child's educational needs, it would be surprising if a document prepared to enable informed decisions to be made about the best educational provisions to meet the particular needs of the child did not permit for some flexibility and sensible interpretation of a document with ongoing significance in the child's life…".

It follows that Section B may lawfully contain some reference to matters which represent narrative account, background, context or even provision, but it must not specify provision, and it should be set out in a fashion which is sufficiently specific and clear so as to leave no room for doubt as to what are the identified SEN which call for special educational provision to be specified in section F.

Further, paragraph 9.61 of the 2015 Code of Practice states that an EHC plan should be 'clear' and 'concise'.

A child or young person has a 'disability' for the purposes of the 2014 Act Part 3 if he or she has a disability for the purposes of the Equality Act 2010: section 83(3) of the 2014 Act.

The SEND Code of Practice provides the following explanation within its introduction section, paragraph xvii, thus: "Many children and young people who have SEN may have a disability under the Equality Act 2010 – that is '...a physical or mental impairment which has a long-term and substantial adverse effect on their ability to carry out normal day-to-day activities'. This definition provides a relatively low threshold and includes more children than many realise: 'long-term' is defined as 'a year or more' and 'substantial' is defined as 'more than minor or trivial'. This definition includes sensory impairments such as those affecting sight or hearing, and long-term health conditions such as asthma, diabetes, epilepsy, and cancer. Children and young people with such conditions do not necessarily have SEN, but there is a significant overlap between disabled children and young people and those with SEN. Where a disabled child or young person requires special educational provision they will also be covered by the SEN definition."

In fact, the Equality Act 2010 provides a complex definition of disability in section 6, which should be read together with section 212(1) and Schedule 1 of the 2010 Act.

There is also statutory guidance issued by the Secretary of State under section 6(5) of the 2010 Act, 'Guidance on matters to be taken into account in determining questions relating to the definition of disability'.

Section 6(1) of the Equality Act 2010 provides: "A person (P) has a disability if— (a) P has a physical or mental impairment, and (b) the impairment has a substantial and long-term adverse effect on P's ability to carry out normal day-to-day activities." 'Long-term' is *not* defined in the 2010 Act as 'year or more'. Rather, Schedule 1, paragraph 2(1) provides that the effect of an impairment is long-term if: (a) it has lasted for at least 12 months, (b) it is likely to last for at least 12 months, or (c) it is likely to last for the rest of the life of the person affected. Paragraph 2(2) provides that if an impairment ceases to have a substantial adverse effect on a person's ability to carry out normal day-to-day activities, it is to be treated as continuing to have that effect if that effect is 'likely' to recur. 'Likely' in the context of paragraph 2 means 'could well': *SCA Packaging Ltd v Boyle* [2009] IRLR 746 HL. For a child or young person to have a disability for the purposes of the Equality Act 2010 and consequently for the purposes of the Children and Families Act 2014, Part 3, it is not necessary to consider how the relevant impairment is *caused* – what is important to consider is the impairment's *effect* (see the statutory guidance, paragraph A7, and *Ministry of Defence v Hay* 2008 ICR 1247, EAT).

The Upper Tribunal has also stated that special educational needs may be accurately assessed without knowing their precise cause: *SG v Denbighshire County Council* [2018] UKUT 369 (AAC) at [40].

The Equality Act 2010 does not require a strict line to be drawn between a learning difficulty and a disability. By way of example, developmental impairments such as autistic spectrum disorder (ASD), dyslexia and dyspraxia, learning disabilities and mental health conditions with symptoms such as anxiety, are referred to in the statutory guidance as examples of impairments which could amount to disabilities for the purposes of the 2010 Act 2010 (see paragraph A5, p. 9 of the statutory guidance).

However, section 20(2)(b) of the 2014 Act applies only to a disability which prevents or hinders the child from making use of "facilities". In *Hertfordshire v MC & KC* [2016] UKUT 385 (AAC) at [14] the Upper Tribunal stated: *"'Facilities' are likely to refer to physical facilities such as the playground, lunch hall, toilets, corridors, and classroom, but seems inapt to cover the way in which the school provides education for the pupil."* It is also important to note that the facilities in question for the purposes of section 20(2)(b) are those of a kind "generally provided for others of the same age in mainstream schools or mainstream post-16 institutions." This is a reference to what is generally provided in England, not to what is generally provided within the area of the relevant local authority. This is a significant change from the definition within the predecessor legislation, the Education Act 1996 section 312, which referred to "educational facilities of a kind generally provided for children of his age in schools within the area of the local authority".

Subsection 20(2)(b) of the 2014 Act, the 'second limb' of subsection 20(2), is sometimes overlooked. However, paragraphs 6.34 and 6.35 of the SEND Code of Practice (set out in full in this Chapter, below) explain how children and young people without learning difficulties, who have sensory and/or physical needs, may have SEN for the purposes of the 2014 Act, Part 3. Notably, paragraph 6.34 contemplates the situation of a child or young person who has sensory and/or physical difficulties which fluctuate over time.

It is worth noting that, in the context of children's social care services, section 17 of the Children Act 1989 (provision of services for children in need, their families and others) provides a different definition of children who are disabled which applies for the purposes of Part III of the 1989 Act.

Paragraphs 6.28 to 6.35 in Chapter 6 of the 2015 Code of Practice provides an outline of four broad areas of need: communication and interaction, cognition and learning, social emotional and mental health difficulties, and sensory and/or physical needs. The Code makes clear, however, that the purpose of providing this overview is not to fit a child or young person into a category: in practice, individual children or young people often have needs that cut across all these areas:

> ***Communication and interaction***
>
> *6.28 Children and young people with speech language and communication needs (SLCN) have difficulty in communicating with others. This may be because they have difficulty saying what they want*

to, understanding what is being said to them or they do not understand or use social rules of communication. The profile for every child with SLCN is different and there needs may change overtime. They may have difficulty with one, some or all of the different aspects of speech, language or social communication at different times of their lives.

6.29 Children and young people with ASD, including Asperger's Syndrome and Autism, are likely to have difficulties with social interaction. They may also experience difficulties with language, communication and imagination, which can impact on how they relate to others.

Cognition and learning

6.30 Support for learning difficulties may be required when children and young people learn at a slower pace than their peers, even with appropriate differentiation. Learning difficulties cover a wide range of needs, including moderate learning difficulties (MLD), severe learning difficulties (SLD), where children are likely to need support in all areas of the curriculum and associated difficulties with mobility and communication, through to profound and multiple learning difficulties (PMLD), where children are likely to have severe and complex learning difficulties as well as a physical disability or sensory impairment.

6.31 Specific learning difficulties (SpLD), affect one or more specific aspects of learning. This encompasses a range of conditions such as dyslexia, dyscalculia and dyspraxia.

Social, emotional and mental health difficulties

6.32 Children and young people may experience a wide range of social and emotional difficulties which manifest themselves in many ways. These may include becoming withdrawn or isolated, as well as displaying challenging, disruptive or disturbing behaviour. These behaviours may reflect underlying mental health difficulties such as anxiety or depression, self-harming, substance misuse, eating disorders

> *or physical symptoms that are medically unexplained. Other children and young people may have disorders such as attention deficit disorder, attention deficit hyperactive disorder or attachment disorder.*
>
> ...
>
> ***Sensory and/or physical needs***
>
> *6.34 Some children and young people require special educational provision because they have a disability which prevents or hinders them from making use of the educational facilities generally provided. These difficulties can be age related and may fluctuate over time. Many children and young people with vision impairment (VI), hearing impairment (HI) or multi-sensory impairment (MSI) will require specialist support and/or equipment to access their learning, or habilitation support...*
>
> *6.35 Some children and young people with a physical disability (PD) require additional ongoing support and equipment to access all the opportunities available to their peers.*

Many if not most local authorities structure Section B of their EHC plans so that the SEN of the child or young person are described under the four headings of communication and interaction, cognition and learning, social emotional and mental health difficulties, and sensory and/or physical needs. However, there is no legal requirement for them to do this, nor is this suggested in the SEND Code of Practice.

Powers of the First-tier Tribunal in 'Section B' appeals, and compliance

By regulation 43(1) of the 2014 Regulations, before determining any appeal, the First-tier Tribunal may, with the agreement of the parties, correct any deficiencies in the EHC Plan which relate to the special educational needs or special educational provision for the child or the young person.

By regulation 43(2)(a) and (f), when determining a 'Section B' appeal, the powers of First-tier Tribunal include the power to dismiss the appeal, or to order the local authority to continue to maintain the EHC Plan with amendments so far as that relates to the SEN. The Tribunal also has a power to make "any other consequential amendments as [it] thinks fit": regulation 42(2)(f). In *S v Worcestershire CC (SEN)* [2017] UKUT 0092 (AAC) at [84-85], in the context of a 'Section F' appeal, the Upper Tribunal held that this meant the Tribunal could make consequential amendments to the outcomes stated in Section E.

By regulation 44(2)(h), where the order requires the local authority to continue and amend an EHC Plan, the LA shall continue to maintain the EHC Plan and amend the EHC Plan within 5 weeks of the order being made. Where the order requires the LA to continue to maintain an EHC Plan in its existing form, the LA shall continue to maintain the EHC Plan (regulation 44(2)(g)). This is subject any direction made by the First-tier Tribunal: regulation 44(1).

In an unopposed appeal, under regulation 45, the Tribunal is not required to make an order. If the appeal is made under section 51(2)(c)(i) or (e) of the 2014 Act, the local authority must issue the amended EHC plan to those specified in regulation 22(3) within 5 weeks of the date it notifies the First-tier Tribunal that it will not oppose the appeal before it submits a response: regulation 45(4).

CHAPTER FIVE

SPECIAL EDUCATIONAL PROVISION AND 'SECTION F' APPEALS

Overview

Sections 20 and 21 of the Children and Families Act 2014 Part 3, which define special educational needs and special education provision, and regulation 12(1)(f) of the Special Educational Needs and Disability Regulations 2014, are the key provisions which govern Section F of EHC plans. Regulation 12(1)(f) provides that when preparing an EHC plan a local authority must set out the special educational provision required by the child or young person in Section F of the plan. Paragraph 9.69 of the Code sets out in tabular format what to include in each section of the EHC plan, including Section F.

Subsections 51(1), (2)(c)(ii) and (e) of the 2014 Act make provision for 'Section F' appeals. A child's parent or a young person may appeal to the First-tier Tribunal against the matters set out in subsection (2), subject to section 55 (mediation). Subsection 51(2)(c)(ii) refers, where an EHC plan is maintained for the child or young person, to the special educational provision specified in the plan. Subsection 51(2)(e) refers to a decision of a local authority not to secure the amendment or replacement of an EHC plan it maintains for the child or young person following a review or re-assessment under section 44. By subsection 51(3), the circumstances in which a parent or young person may bring an appeal under subsection 51(2(c) are when an EHC plan is first finalised (s. 51(3)(a)) and following an amendment or replacement of the plan (s. 51(3)(b)). Regulations 18 to 28 of the 2014 Regulations deal with reviewing, re-assessing, amending and replacing EHC plans.

Section 21 of the 2014 Act defines "special educational provision" as well as "health care provision" and "social care provision" for the purposes of Part 3, and states:

> 21 Special educational provision, health care provision and social care provision
>
> (1) "Special educational provision", for a child aged two or more or a young person, means educational or training provision that is additional to, or different from, that made generally for others of the same age in—
>
> (a) mainstream schools in England,
>
> (b) maintained nursery schools in England,
>
> (c) mainstream post-16 institutions in England, or
>
> (d) places in England at which relevant early years education is provided.
>
> (2) "Special educational provision", for a child aged under two, means educational provision of any kind.
>
> (3) "Health care provision" means the provision of health care services as part of the comprehensive health service in England continued under section 1(1) of the National Health Service Act 2006.
>
> (4) "Social care provision" means the provision made by a local authority in the exercise of its social services functions.
>
> (5) Health care provision or social care provision which educates or trains a child or young person is to be treated as special educational provision (instead of health care provision or social care provision).
>
> (6) This section applies for the purposes of this Part.

This means that the following provision must be specified in Section F: (a) special educational provision as defined by section 21(1) or 21(2); (b) health care services provided as part of the comprehensive health service in England continued under section 1(1) of the National Health Service Act 2006, if they "educate or train" the child or young person; (c) provision made by a local authority in the exercise of its social services functions, if it "educates or trains" the child or young person.

Regulations 12(1)(c), (d), (g) and (h) of the 2014 Regulations, which relate to the specification of other social care and health care needs and provision, are considered further in Chapter 9 which addresses 'extended appeals'.

As for what "educational" means for the purposes of section 21, and what "educates or trains" means for the purposes of sub-section 21(5), there is a substantial body of case law relevant to these questions. Some of this arises from appeals where parents argued that therapies such physiotherapy, occupational therapy or speech and language therapy, normally obtained through health care providers, were special educational provision. Other case law arises from appeals where parents argued that their child needed to learn 'life skills', for example, learning how to feed or dress or communicate. In more recent appeals concerning young people, including those aged 19-25 years, appellants have argued that the young person in question needed to learn skills for independent living. Other case law arises from appeals where parents argued that their child needed help so that they could attend or function at school, for example a wheelchair or lift at school, or medical or personal care at school during the school day. Some of this case law is looked at in this Chapter, below.

By section 38(2) of the 2014 Act and regulation 12(1)(f) of the 2014 Regulations, Section F must specify the special educational provision "required" by the child or young person. This has been interpreted in case law to mean what is "reasonably required": *A v Hertfordshire County Council* [2006] EWHC 3428 at [25]. It follows that provision which is merely 'recommended' should not be specified. A fuller look at the relevant case law is provided in in this Chapter, below.

Paragraph 9.61 of the 2015 Code of Practice states that EHC plans should be 'clear, concise, understandable and accessible to parents, children, young people, providers and practitioners. They should be written so they can be understood by professionals in any local authority'. Provision in Section F must be 'so specific and so clear as to leave no room for doubt as to what has been decided and what is needed in the individual case": *L v Clarke and Somerset* [1998] ELR 129 at [27]. The question, whether the provision in section F is sufficiently specific and clear, is a common issue in Section F appeals. The case law relevant to the issue of 'specificity' looked at further in this Chapter, below.

It is now not uncommon for 'Section F' appeals to relate to: Speech and Language Therapy, other therapies such Physiotherapy or Occupational Therapy, teaching in small groups of pupils or small classes, teaching out of year group, special educational provision outside of the normal school or college day, sometimes referred to as a 'waking day curriculum' and education otherwise than in a school (or college).

Education otherwise than at school (or college) is a substantial subject which spans section F and section I appeals and is addressed in Chapter 7.

What is meant by "required"?

In A v Hertfordshire County Council [2006] EWHC 3428 at [25]. Gilbert J considered the question thus:

> "It was common ground... that the phrase "special educational needs" did not encompass every form of activity or therapy which could achieve some benefit. As it was put in argument, a child is not entitled to "Rolls Royce" provision. But I have found limited assistance from counsel's arguments on how one applies that sensible precept. That is not their fault. The difficulty is caused by the use of, if I may say so, the very slippery word "need" in the Act.

> What is "needed" depends on the question one asks. Is what is to be sought for [the child] that she achieves the maximum degree of progress that is attainable or a lesser but still substantial one? If the former, then the "need" will require the provision to meet the maximum. If the latter – i.e. the lesser but still substantial degree of progress – then the "need" may require less provision. Suppose that the evidence were that a child with special educational needs had development objectives which required speech and language therapy. The evidence showed that 16 hours per month would achieve little, whereas 25 hours would achieve a great deal. What if 27 hours per month would achieve a better result? Would there be a failure then within the meaning of section 324 if the Local Education Authority provided for 25 as opposed to 27 hours? In my judgment, the way in which this issue must be addressed is to interpret the section on the basis that when it refers to "needs" it is referring to "what is reasonably required". That means that a decision can and must be made on whether what is being proposed for inclusion in a Statement of Educational Needs is reasonably required or goes beyond that. That is pre-eminently a matter for the expert judgment of the Tribunal."

In *Devon County Council v OH* [2016] 0282 (AAC) Ward J held, at [33], that *A v Hertfordshire* continued to be relevant under the 2014 Act and also expressly held, at [38], that although subsection 37(2)(c) of the 2014 Act refers to the special educational provision that is "required" whereas subsections 37(2)(d) and (f) refer to health care and social care provision that "reasonably required", this should not be interpreted as meaning that special educational provision is not subject to a limitation that it be "reasonably" required.

Consideration of sections B and I in 'Section F' appeals

Section F must be written with reference to what the child or young person 'reasonably requires', not to what the school or other institution named (or likely to be named) in Section I can offer. In *R v. Kingston*

Upon Thames Council and Hunter [1997] ELR 223 McCullough J stated the principle as follows (at p. 9):

> "... Part 4 cannot influence Part 3. It is not a matter of fitting Part 3 to Part 4 but of considering the fitness of Part 4 to meet the provision in Part 3."

In *A v Barnet LBC* [2003] EWHC 3368 at [17] the High Court (Lloyd Jones QC) restated this principle: "it is the duty of a local education authority to decide first what are a child's special educational needs within Part 2, secondly what special educational provision is necessary to meet those needs within Part 3 and thirdly to make an appropriate placement within Part 4. These questions have to be addressed in this order because it is only when a decision has been taken as to a child's special educational needs that it is possible to decide what provision is required to meet them. Similarly, it is only when a decision has been taken as to the necessary provision that it is possible to decide which school can make that provision..."

In *The Learning Trust v MP* [2007] EWHC 1634 (Admin), [2007] ELR 658 at the High Court (Nicol QC) stated, at [42], that Parts 2 and 3 of a statement have been likened to a medical diagnosis and prescription: R *v Secretary of State for Education and Science ex parte E* [1992] 1 FLR 377, 388-389. It is important then to identify or diagnose the need before going on to prescribe the educational provision to which that need gives rise, and only once the necessary educational provision has been identified can one specify the institution or type of institution which is appropriate to provide it. However, Nicol QC added, "I bear in mind that one cannot be over-prescriptive in this regard. If it is clear, for instance, that a residential school is necessary to meet an identified educational need, the precise form of the provision can be influenced by what is available at a particular school – see *S v City and Council of Swansea* [1999] ELR 315, at 323."

In *S v City and Council of Swansea* Sullivan J stated:

> "...Whilst the content of Part 3 of the Statement must not be dictated by a prior decision as to placement in Part 4 (that would be to put the cart before the horse), it would be unrealistic to suggest that the Tribunal was not entitled to be "influenced" in its findings as to the amendments to be made to Part 3 by its decision as to the P school. The prescription in Part 3 of a Statement has to be delivered in the real world by a particular school or schools: see the judgment of Harrison J in *R v Secretary of State for Education, ex parte W (unreported)* Transcript, dated 27th May 1994.
>
> Provided it is appropriate to meet the needs specified in Part 2 and the objectives specified in Part 3, the prescription in the remainder of Part 3 may be "informed" by what is actually available at a particular school. It is, however, a corollary of this approach, that if a particular school is to be relied upon to meet a particular need, the tribunal must have accurately defined the need in Part 2 and must have been able to satisfy itself that the school will be able to provide the special educational provision specified in the Statement: see again Harrison J at pages 13 to 14 of *ex parte W*."

Where there is consensus that the school or type of school to be specified in Section I will be a special school, a lower degree of specificity in section F *might* be appropriate: *S v SENDIST* [2007] EWHC 1139 at [36]; *East Sussex County Council v TW* [2016] UKUT 0528 (ACC), at [41] and *E v Newham LBC* [2003] ELR 286 at [65]. It may be argued that this would be an exception to the general rule that 'Section I cannot influence Section F'.

What does "educational" mean for the purposes of subsections 21(1) and (2), and what does "educates or trains" mean for the purposes of sub-section 21(5)?

By virtue of section 83(2) of the 2014 Act and section 15ZA(8) of the Education Act 1996, "training" includes full-time and part-time training, apprenticeship training, and (by section 15ZA8(b)) "vocational, social, physical and recreational training".

An appropriate starting point in the case law is *London Borough of Bromley v Special Educational Needs Tribunal & Others* [1999] ELR 260. This established that the question, whether a particular form of provision needed by the child or young person is "educational", is one which must be decided by the local authority, or, upon an appeal, the First-tier Tribunal, exercising a case-by-case judgment; Parliament has declined to provide a statutory definition.

The appeal in *Bromley* arose out of a conclusion by the SEN Tribunal that the child's need for physiotherapy, occupational therapy and speech and language therapy formed part of his SEN, with the consequence that the provision of these therapies was part of the special educational provision which the LEA had to make for him. The central issue before the Court of Appeal was the meaning and ambit of "special educational provision" in Part IV of the Education Act 1996. Sedley LJ observed that the SEN Tribunal was a specialist tribunal. He also observed that, for the purpose of making a statement under section 324 of the 1996 Act, an LEA was required to distinguish between 'special educational provision' and 'non-educational provision'. He held:

> "Two possibilities arise here: either the two categories share a common frontier, so that where the one stops the other begins; or there is between the unequivocally educational and the unequivocally non-educational a shared territory of provision which can be intelligibly allocated to either… to adopt the first approach would be to read into the legislation a sharp dichotomy for which Parliament could easily have made express provision had it wished to do so, but which finds no expression or reflection where one would expect to find it, namely in s 312. Moreover, to interpose a hard edge or a common frontier does not get rid of definitional problems: it simply makes them more acute. And this is one of the reasons why… the second approach is the one to be attributed to Parliament. The potentially large intermediate area of provision which is capable of ranking as educational or non-educational is not made the subject of any statutory prescription precisely because it is for the local education authority, and if necessary the SENT, to exercise a case-by-case judgment which no

> prescriptive legislation could ever hope to anticipate… Whether a form of help needed by the child falls within this description is a question primarily for the LEA and secondarily for the SENT's expert judgment. If, but only if, the SENT has gone wrong in law will the High Court overset its judgment."

A v Hertfordshire County Council [2006] EWHC 3428, concerned a child, 'D', with very severe learning difficulties whose family wanted her to attend a residential school. The Court (Gilbart QC) observed at [22] that 'D' needed to learn all those life skills which the educational system provided for those without SEN assumed that she had, but, of course, learning how to feed and communicate was as vital to her as the ability to divide and multiply would be to a child of the same age without special needs. Getting 'D' to learn how to put her coat on, for example, which involved getting her to do it again and again, might be very difficult to distinguish from simply helping her put her coat on, a normal incident of care. How is the line to be drawn in cases of overlap, or is one to be drawn at all? It was argued for the parents that anything which helped D learn what to do was to be regarded as education, and she should be looked after on a 24-hour basis, therefore such provision was (a) educational, and (b) must be provided. The Court considered, at [26], that this went too far: it would mean that every time D was assisted to any degree which in fact helped her learn by repetition, that amounted to educational provision, and that the LEA was required to provide it throughout her waking day. The Court regarded that as unrealistic as a firm rule from which no departure could ever be permitted. Whether a particular case called for it would be a matter for judgment on the facts of that case, and not a matter for a prescriptive rule. It was pre-eminently a matter of fact and degree, and whether it applied in D's case was a matter for expert judgment.

East Sussex CC v TW [2016] UKUT 0528 (ACC), was an appeal under the 2014 Act which concerned a young person registered at a specialist independent college on a day placement who lived in a rented flat with domiciliary support provided by a commissioned care provider. It was argued on his behalf that he required educational programmes during and outside of the normal college day relating to behavioural management, daily living skills and the development of social skills and friendships. At [15-25], Jacobs J considered the operation of section 21 of the 2014 Act and regulation 12 of the 2014 Regulations insofar as they related to special educational provision and social care provision in the EHC plan. Subsections 21(1) and (2) define special educational provision as provision that is in addition to or different from that generally made for others of the same age in, for that case, mainstream post-16 institutions. This goes into Section F of the plan: regulation 12(1)(f). Subsection 21(4) deals with social care provision by defining it as provision made by the local authority in the exercise of its social services functions. This goes into Section D of the plan: regulation 12(1)(d). Section 21(5) operates in respect of that part of the person's social care that *also* educates or trains; does not apply to *all* social care, regardless of its effect. TW might need some social care in respect of his back problems, for example, but that part of his social care package did not become special education provision just because other parts of the package 'educated or trained' him. The result of subsection 21(5) is that the parts of the social care package which educated or trained TW became special educational provision to be specified in Section F of the plan and not in Section D, and the LA had to secure the provision under section 42(2). Jacobs J further stated at [24] that when a case comes before the First-tier Tribunal, the local authority may already have applied section 21(5) but if not, the Tribunal must apply it and, if necessary, move the relevant provision from Section D to Section F.

It seems likely that when referring to section D in these passages, the intended reference was to section H.

As *East Sussex CC v TW* was decided before the introduction of the First-Tier Tribunal by the Special Educational Needs and Disability (First-tier Tribunal Recommendations Power) Regulations 2017, the Tribunal had no power to influence in any way the provision that remained social care provision under section 21(4). The 2017 Regulations are further explained in this book in Chapter 9.

In *GL v West Sussex CC* [2017] UKUT 414 (AAC) a question arose whether social care provision to improve the young person's ability to 'generalise' skills learnt at college in out of college time was education or training in such skills and so special educational provision by virtue of section 21(5). Wikeley J, at [32], analysed the question as being whether the social care provision in question falls on the "education or training" side of the line or the "support" side of the line and confirmed that this is a question for the specialist Tribunal to determine in the light of its own expertise. Following *A v Hertfordshire County Council*, this is ultimately a question of fact and degree: "One cannot simply work from the premise that any support which helps a young person learn what to do is necessarily to be regarded as a form of education (or training)."

Wikeley J further stated, at [16-20] and [33], that, in keeping with the Explanatory Notes to the 2014 Act, he did not regard section 21(5) as in any way marking a departure from the principles established in the pre-2014 Act case law. There has long been acknowledged to be an overlap between the provision of education and care. It is only social care provision that "educates or trains" which is to be treated as special educational provision under section 21(5) (or as Jacobs J termed it in *East Sussex County Council v TW* 'deemed special educational provision'). Whether the social care provision "educates or trains" or merely supports or assists is ultimately a factual assessment for the specialist Tribunal.

Paragraphs 169 and 170 of the Explanatory Notes to the 2014 Act state that the definitions of health and social care provision in section 21 reflects the precedents set by case law in relation to the current SEN legislation, and that section 21 replicates, and replaces in England, the current definition of special educational provision in section 312 of the 1996 Act and applies it to young people over compulsory school age.

East Sussex County Council v KS (SEN) [2017] UKUT 273 concerned a girl, 'L', who had a range of complex medical needs as well as special educational needs. Her parents wanted her to attend a non-maintained special school for children and young people with complex neuro disabilities, high health needs and associated learning difficulties ('CHS'). The matter came before the Upper Tribunal because the CHS school fees contained an element for 'clinical services', the relevant clinical commissioning group refused to pay this element on the grounds that the clinical services required by L were available via universal services, and the local authority argued it had no power to pay this element because it did not constitute 'educational' provision. Section 63(2) of the 2014 Act requires the LA to "pay any fees payable in respect of education or training provided for the child or young person at that school, institution or place in accordance with the EHC plan". The "responsible commissioning body" has the legal duty to arrange the health care provision specified in section G of the plan (subsections 42(3) and (4) of the 2014 Act), but also the legal power to determine what that provision should be (regulation 12(2) of the 2014 Regulations).

Ward J held, at [89], that "even if medical and nursing support is ... essential for [the child] to be educated, that does not of itself make it special educational provision", although such support could come within subsection 21(5) if the specific requirements of that subsection are met. In so stating, Ward J had considered the authorities of *City of Bradford v A* [1996] CO 3788/95, *R v Lambeth ex p MBM* [1995] and *OD v Gloucestershire CC* [2013] UKUT 112.

In *City of Bradford v A*, Brooke J considered *R v Lancashire CC Ex p. CM (A Minor)* [1989] 2 FLR 279, [1989] 3 WLUK 132, in which it was held that teaching a child to communicate by speech was no different from teaching him to communicate by writing and both were educational and so the provision of speech therapy was special educational provision. Brooke J held that nursing care was a non-educational provision and therefore it was not within the remit of the Tribunal to amend Part 3 of the statement to specify nursing care for 100 per cent of the time A was at school; this was not a case where the provision was on the borderline between educational and non-educational as in the case of speech therapy. In *R v Lambeth ex p MBM* Owen J held that the provision of a lift to enable a disabled child to access facilities on the first floor of her school could not be regarded as provision for an educational need under the Education Act 1993 section 168(5); installation of a lift would be to assist the child's mobility and not her educational needs. *OD v Gloucestershire* concerned a child in relation to whom there were repeated problems getting him to leave the car which took him to school and go into the school, so he became a boarder at the school following which his attendance had improved. The local authority did not consider that a statement was needed. Parents argued that the child's emotional problems which hindered him from attending a day school were SEN within section 312 of the 1996 Act, because they hindered him making use of the school's educational facilities and this called for special educational provision to be made for him in the form of a boarding school. The Tribunal concluded that a boarding school was not called for and that the appropriate course was for the problem to be addressed by the Child and Adolescent Mental Health Services of the NHS (CAMHS). Mark J held that the Tribunal was entitled to conclude that a re-referral to CAMHS was the way in which the problem ought to be addressed at this stage and not by special educational provision in the form of boarding school.

In East Sussex County Council v JC [2018] UKUT 81 (AAC) the dispute centred on whether the provision of a powered wheelchair was or was not in itself educational provision. It was argued on behalf of the young person ('W') that a powered wheelchair was an essential tool for all aspects of W's life and that without the wheelchair he could not access education, make expected progress and attain the expected outcomes in relation to his independence. Levenson J stated, at [31]: "... I am not satisfied that [the Tribunal] made adequate findings and gave an adequate explanation as to how [W]'s use of the wheelchair actually educates or trains him. Is it because learning to use it, and developing and applying that learning, in itself amounts to education or training? If so, is this a one-off process that only takes a very short time, like learning to make a cup of tea? Is it an ongoing, developing and cumulative process, like learning computer skills? Is there nothing to learn in this process but only from the facilities that the wheelchair enables [W] to travel to?"

In *DC & DC v Hertfordshire County Council* [2016] UKUT 379 (AAC) Lane J provided some further guidance (at [15-18]) when considering whether the 'support of a psychiatrist' can be categorised as special educational provision. There is 'no bright line test to determine whether provision is educational or not' but the definition of education as 'systematic instruction, schooling or training' provides 'some light': at [15]. If a form of provision relates to a matter within the curriculum, there will probably be little doubt that provision is educational, but even provision requiring the adaptation of a school's physical environment may constitute educational provision; an example would be the provision of a low noise or low distraction environment for a pupil with a sensory disorder: at [16]. Education, although it may be very wide ranging in concept, is about instruction, schooling or training, so one or more of these factors is likely to be discernible in provision which is asserted to be educational. The provision should be directly related to the pupil's learning difficulty or disability (see *H v A London Borough* SEN) [2015] UKUT 0316 (AAC)), should relate to a specified educational objective and it should be possible to see what the provision is trying to instil, teach or train the pupil to do. There may be teaching strategies or learning strategies built into the provision. Where the provision directly requires pupil participation, the provision may indicate how it will be encouraged, rewarded or otherwise. One would expect some outcomes to be built in: at [17]. A few examples may be contrasted. (i) A SSEN provides mindfulness training for a pupil with an anxiety disorder. The objective is to enable the pupil to remain calm, keep focussed in class and relate to other children at playtime. Mindfulness is based on principles and practice to secure what is learned. (ii) The same pupil is also provided with cognitive behavioural therapy to teach him how to deal with anxiety that pops up suddenly. (iii) The pupil also undergoes hypnosis regularly to help him stop self-harming. In the first two examples, the child is receiving systematic training and learning coping strategies to help him learn in the classroom and learn to get along with fellow pupils, as a member of the school community. Both appear to be educational. In the third example the child is being 'practiced upon' in order to change his behaviour. His behaviour is affected 'subliminally'. It may be thought unlikely that this would be educational provision any more than taking an anti-biotic for a sore throat: at [18].

H v A London Borough, referred to in *DC & DC v Hertfordshire County Council* above, was an appeal in which Ward J, at [28b], accepted that the First-tier Tribunal had been entitled to find that the child's sexually harmful behaviour was not part of his learning difficulty; the question was the special educational provision which was called for by what the Tribunal *had* found to be his learning difficulty.

In *EAM v East Sussex County Council* [2022] UKUT 193 (AAC) Jacobs J stated at paragraphs [8-10] that 'educational provision' as in section 21(1) and provision 'which educates or trains' as in section 21(5) are different and not interchangeable. Authorities on the latter should not be treated as relevant to the former. A provision may be educational without itself educating a child. By way of example, a teacher may give a lesson to a class which includes a pupil who has impaired hearing and wears a hearing aid. The school has installed a loop system and the teacher uses a microphone so that, with the hearing aid on the T setting, the pupil can hear the lesson. The microphone and the loop system are both educational provision, but they do not themselves educate the pupil. The hearing aid may be an educational provision *and* a health care provision, but again it does not educate the pupil. The teacher and the contents of the lesson educate the pupil. It is only relevant to decide whether a provision 'educates or trains' a child or young person if it is also health or social care provision.

It is relevant to note the provisions of section 100 of the 2014 Act ('Duty to support pupils with medical conditions'), which sits outside Part 3 of the 2014 but within the "Education Acts" as listed in section 578(1) of the 1996 Act. Section 100 places a duty on the governing body of a maintained school or a pupil referral unit or the proprietor of an Academy school or alternative provision Academy to make arrangements for supporting pupils at the school with medical conditions and, in meeting the duty, must have regard to guidance issued by the Secretary of State. The Department of Education has produced statutory guidance for governing bodies of maintained schools and proprietors of academies in England, "Supporting pupils at school with medical conditions".

Provision by parents and privately paid carers

Section F must only specify provision which is special educational provision as defined in section 21, and subsection 42(2) requires the local authority to secure the special educational provision specified in Section F unless the child's parent or the young person has made suitable alternative arrangements: subsection 42(5). It follows that if the SEN of the child or young person calls for the provision of, for example, specialist communication skills training in the home, the LA would not be performing its statutory duty if, when specifying special educational provision in section F, it directly or indirectly imposed an obligation to meet all or part of that provision upon the parent: *A v Cambridgeshire* [2002] EWHC 2391 at [60]. In *TW and KW v Hampshire County Council* (SEN) [2022] UKUT 305 (AAC) Ward J, applying *A v Cambridgeshire,* held that a plan which specified a person's privately-funded carers to make provision in section F was not lawful: at [27-28]. The distinction drawn by the High Court (Gilbart QC) in *A v Hertfordshire County Council* [2006] EWHC 3428, at [22], between care which helps a child to learn, and educational provision, is relevant here.

However, meetings between parent and teacher, when requested by the parent, might, on the correct set of facts, amount to special educational provision (see further, *HN v South Tyneside Council (SEN)* [2019] UKUT 380 (AAC) at [31], below).

Quality first teaching

SEND Code of Practice 2015 states at paragraph 6.37, "High quality teaching, differentiated for individual pupils, is the first step in responding to pupils who have or may have SEN…" Such provision would not constitute special educational provision, where it is not "additional to, or different from, that made generally for others of the same age in mainstream schools in England" as per subsection 21(1) of the 2014 Act.

Speech and language therapy

It is well established that speech and language therapy can be regarded as special educational provision: *R v Lancashire CC ex parte M [1989] 2 FLR 279*; *X&X v Caerphilly Borough Council* [2004] EWHC 2140. Paragraph 9.74 of the 2015 Code of Practice states: "Decisions about whether health care provision or social care provision **must** be made on an individual basis. Speech and language therapy and other therapy provision can be regarded as either education or health care provision, or both. It could therefore be included in an EHC plan as either educational or health provision. However, since communication is so fundamental in education, addressing speech and language impairment should normally be recorded as special educational provision unless there are exceptional reasons for not doing so."

Placement in a different year group

In *AB v North Somerset Council* [2010] UKUT 8 (AAC) the Upper Tribunal held, at [28], that the allocation of a child to a different year group fell within the definition of special educational provision.

"Reasonable adjustments"

In *RB v Calderdale MBC (SEN)* [2022] UKUT 136 (AAC) Rowley J considered whether a Tribunal dealing with a 'Section F' appeal should consider the reasonable adjustments required for the child or young person under the Equality Act 2010. The short answer to that question was "no": at [2]. The longer answer (at [46-49]) was that both statutes have a shared aim of removing barriers to learning and the issue of whether a child or young person has a disability for the purposes of Part 3 of the 2014 Act is determined by reference to whether they have a disability for the purposes of the 2010 Act but that is as far as it goes. Under the 2014 Act a local authority is responsible for making provision for a pupil's SEN (section 42). In contrast, under the 2010 Act, the duty to make reasonable adjustments is placed on the responsible body of a school (section 85). In practice, the SEN framework may result in provision which could also be viewed as auxiliary aids and services under the 2010 Act. By way of example, taken from the Equality and Human Rights Commission's Technical Guidance on Reasonable Adjustments for Disabled Pupils, 2015, a disabled pupil who has an EHC plan and attends a maintained mainstream secondary school may, through her EHC plan, receive two hours a week of specialist teaching and use an electronic notetaker in lessons. Because the support that she requires is provided through her EHC plan, the school does not have to make reasonable adjustments by providing these auxiliary aids and services for her. However, it does not follow that a Tribunal deciding an SEN appeal under the 2014 Act must simultaneously consider reasonable adjustments for the child or young person under the provisions of the 2010 Act.

A non-mainstream peer group

In *A J v London Borough of Croydon* [2020] UKUT 246 (AAC) Counsel accepted that placement in a non-mainstream peer group was special educational provision and, at [52], West J stated that that concession was rightly made in light of what the Upper Tribunal had said in *AB v North Somerset Council* [2010] UKUT 8 (AAC) about the analogous question of the placement of the child in a different year group.

Meetings and liaison

It is not uncommon, where Section F specifies therapy such as speech and language therapy, for it also to specify meeting time between the therapist, school staff and other professionals. However, it should be clear how such meetings would provide something of educational worth for the child, for example discussion of strategies that school staff would put in place for the child, and that they are reasonably required.

In *HN v South Tyneside Council (SEN)* [2019] UKUT 380 (AAC), parents wanted section F to specify twice termly face to face meetings between parents and a teacher of the child at his school. Wright J stated, at [31], that meetings between parent and teacher *might*, on the correct set of facts, amount to special educational provision, if the child's difficulties arising from their disabilities or learning difficulties in attending and integrating into the school or class on school days were such that they needed very close and regular liaison between the child's parents and class teacher, for example in the form of daily discussions about strategies the parents could put in place at home or on the journey to school, in order to enable the child to access their education; such cases are likely to be rare if not very rare.

Residential placements, educational provision outside of the normal school/college day and "Waking day curriculum"

In practice, a child (or young person) may need to attend a school (or college) as a boarder because there is no suitable/appropriate school (or college) within a reasonable distance of their home which they could attend on a day basis. However, there is recognition in the case law that provision in a residential setting can constitute special educational provision of itself. There is also recognition in the case law that a child or young person may need special educational provision outside of the normal school or college day which may or may not need to be delivered in a residential placement. Sometimes this is referred to a 'waking day curriculum'. This case law is considered below.

OD v Gloucestershire CC [2013] UKUT 112 concerned a child in relation to whom there were repeated problems getting him to leave the car which took him to school and go into the school, and who became a boarder at the school which substantially improved his attendance. The premise of the parent's case, that special educational provision could take the form of boarding school, was not doubted, although Mark J held that the Tribunal was entitled to find on the facts of the case that it was not required.

The term 'waking day curriculum' has no legal meaning, and it is arguable that there is little consensus among educational professionals as to its meaning either. In *East Sussex County Council v TW* [2016] UKUT 528 (AAC) at [28-30] Jacobs J stated, "As I understand it, it means only that the person's special educational needs are such that they call for special educational provision to be delivered beyond 'normal hours'."

Paragraphs [18-19] of Lane J's decision in *London Borough of Hammersmith and Fulham v JH* [2012] UKUT 328 (AAC) give an indication of the kind of circumstances in which the term 'waking day curriculum' typically arises. A pupil's SEN may mean that he is unable to 'generalise' skills from the classroom to other environments, unlike other pupils without SEN, and requires education outside 'normal hours' in other environments. A pupil may need to have therapies and activities outside of school hours which enable him to develop the skills of daily living (see *LB Bromley v SENDIST* [1999] ELR 260 CA) and to 'translate into his home and social and indeed all areas of his life and functioning, the skill which he learns within the school and school room' (see *S v Solihull MBC* [2007] EWHC 1139 at [17] and [19]). The Tribunal must, therefore, decide whether an extended educational programme continuing after the end of the school day is reasonably required. Jacobs J stated, at [28] in *East Sussex CC v TW*, that this may be linked with residential placement, but that is not necessarily so. For example, independent living skills may be best acquired outside a formal educational setting, when attempting to live independently.

However, the need for consistency of approach beyond the normal school day is not the same as a need for an educational programme beyond the normal school day: *The Learning Trust v SENDIST and MP* [2007] EWHC 1634 (Admin) at [40-41]. In *R (Tottman) v Hertfordshire County Council* [2003] EWHC 1725 (Admin) and *T v Hertfordshire County Council* [2004] EWCA Civ 927 it was agreed that there needed to be consistency of approach and liaison between school and home, but the High Court (Moses J) and the Court of Appeal rejected parents' argument that the statement of special educational needs was deficient because it did not spell out in more detail what was to happen outside school. The fact that a Tribunal identifies that a consistency of approach is required going beyond the normal school day does not mean this is necessarily an educational need nor that it can only be met by way of residential provision: *R (TS) v Bowen and Bowen (Chair of SENDIST) and Solihull MBC* [2009] EWHC 5 (Admin) at [39]. In *Hampshire CC v JP* [2009] UKUT 239 (AAC) at [29] the Upper Tribunal held that in the context of that case, where the issue was whether the child's need for consistency required a residential placement on educational grounds or not, the question was whether his need for consistency was such that his education could not reasonably be provided unless he were accommodated on the site where he was educated.

In *A v Hertfordshire County Council* [2006] EWHC 3428, the High Court (Gilbart QC) held, at [22-26], that although the child might be helped to learn life skills by assistance which was the normal incidence of care, it did not follow that whenever the child was assisted to any degree which in fact helped her learn by repetition, that amounted to educational provision, and that the LEA was required to provide it throughout her waking day: that was pre-eminently a matter of fact and degree, and whether it applied in that child's case was a matter for expert judgment. In *GL v West Sussex CC (SEN)* [2017] UKUT 414 (AAC), which concerned a young person at college, Wikeley J held, at [32], that it is not sufficient to say that social care provision to improve the young person's ability to generalise skills learnt at college in out of college time is, by definition, education or training in such skills and so special educational provision by virtue of section 21(5). "Rather, that is to beg the question, the question being whether the social care provision in question falls on the "education or training" side of the line or the "support" side of the line. That is a question for the specialist Tribunal to determine in the light of its own expertise."

Jacobs J observed, *in London Borough of Southwark v WE* [2021] UKUT 241 (AAC) at [12], that an argument for a waking day curriculum straddles Sections F and I. Whether it is required is part of the analysis of special educational provision. Whether the provision for the curriculum requires a residential placement is part of the analysis of placement. A residential placement is not necessarily required to deliver a waking day curriculum.

<u>Transport</u>

A local authority's duties to arrange home to school (or home to college) transport are set out in Part IX Chapter II of the 1996 Act which deals with ancillary functions of local authorities. The provisions relating to transport in that Chapter are detailed, and an explanation of them lies outside the scope of this book.

In *Staffordshire County Council v JM (SEN)* [2016] UKUT 246 (AAC) Lane J considered, at [24] the authorities of *R v London Bourgh of Havering ex parte K* [1998] ELR 402 at [404-405] (in which Sedley J held that transport under section 509 of the 1996 Act was non-educational provision); *Dudley MBC v JS* [2011] UKUT 67 at [32], which was approved by the Court of Appeal in *Dudley MBC v JS* [2012] EWCA Civ 346; and *MM v DM v London Borough of Harrow* [2010] UKUT 395 (AAC) (in which Jacobs J held, at [27] and [29], that transport is not an educational need; the journey is not part of the children's education; it does not have to provide an opportunity to meet social or educational needs, it is merely a means of getting the children from their homes to their school). Lane J concluded, at [27] of *Staffordshire*, that transport to and from school is neither a special educational need nor special educational provision to meet such a need.

However, Levenson J held in *Birmingham City Council v KF* [2018] UKUT 261 at [19] that home to school transport *is* capable of being special educational provision *if* it educates or trains the child or young person as per section 21(5) of the 2014 Act. It is for an appellant to make the case that the transport fulfils some educational or training function or for the Tribunal to consider this pursuant to its 'inquisitorial' function. The answer will depend on the facts of the particular case.

Writing section F and 'specificity'

Paragraph 9.69 of the Code sets out in tabular format what to include in each section of the EHC plan, including section F. Provision must be detailed and specific and should normally be quantified, for example, in terms of the type, hours and frequency of support and level of expertise, including where this support is secured through a personal budget. In some cases, flexibility will be required to meet the changing needs of the child or young person including flexibility in the use of a Personal Budget. The plan should specify any appropriate facilities and equipment, staffing arrangements and curriculum, any appropriate modifications to the application of the National Curriculum, where relevant, any appropriate exclusions from the application of the National Curriculum or the course being studied in a post-16 setting, in detail, and the provision which it is proposed to substitute for any such exclusions in order to maintain a balanced and broadly based curriculum. Where residential accommodation is appropriate, that fact. Where there is a Personal Budget, the outcomes to which it is intended to contribute (detail of the arrangements for a Personal Budget, including any direct payment, must be included in the plan and these should be set out in section J). Provision must be specified for each and every need specified in section B. It should also be clear how the provision will support achievement of the outcomes in section E. There should be clarity as to how advice and information gathered has informed the provision specified. Where the local authority has departed from that advice, they should say so and give reasons for it.

Provision in Section F must be "so specific and so clear as to leave no room for doubt as to what has been decided is necessary in the individual case": *L v Clarke and Somerset* [1998] ELR 129 at [27], approved by the Court of Appeal in *E v Newham LBC* [2003] ELR 286 at [30].

The Court of Appeal in *E v Newham LBC* [2003] ELR 286 at [64] held that, at one extreme, a Tribunal cannot delegate its statutory duty to some other person or body, however well-qualified, and equally, the statutory duty will not be discharged if the description of the special educational provision which is to be made is framed in terms so vague and uncertain that one cannot discern from it what (if anything) the Tribunal has decided in that respect. At the other extreme, the statutory duty cannot extend to requiring a Tribunal to 'specify' (in the sense of identify or particularise) every last detail of the special educational provision to be made. Between those two extremes, the degree of flexibility which is appropriate in 'specifying' the special educational provision to be made in any particular case is essentially a matter for the Tribunal, taking into account all relevant factors. In some cases, a high degree of flexibility may be appropriate, in others not.

The broad general principles laid down by the Court of Appeal in *E v Newham LBC* must be applied to the particular circumstances of each case as they arise. The contents of Section F have to be as specific and quantified as is necessary and appropriate in any particular case or in any particular aspect of a case, but the emphasis is on the EHC plan being a realistic and practical document which in its nature must allow for a balancing out and adjustment of the various forms of provision specified as knowledge and experience develops on all sides. Wisdom lies also in leaving a wide scope to the expert judgment of the members of the First-tier Tribunal: *CL v Hampshire CC (SEN)* [2011] UKUT 468 (AAC) at [15]. The Tribunal is entitled to delete provision which it considers to be *too* prescriptive: *FC v Suffolk CC* [2010] UKUT 368 (AAC) at [33].

Sullivan J in *S v Swansea CC* [2000] ELR 315 stated, at p.327H, that if the parties' contentions lack particularity, the Tribunal may describe what it decides in less specific terms, but a more detailed dispute may call for more detailed provision. However, the Upper Tribunal stated in *EC v North East Lincolnshire* [2015] UKUT 648 (AAC) at [28] that a Tribunal should not "rubber stamp" a statement of special educational needs that is inadequate and vague on the 'who, what, when and how long' details that are meant to spell out the local authority's duties to the statemented pupil.

In distinguishing between cases where provision is sufficiently specific and those where it is not, it is important that the plan should not be counter-productive or hamper rather than help the provision which is appropriate for a child. The plan has to provide not just for the moment it is made, but for the future as well. If absolute precision is required, it can only be obtained by a continual process of revision of the plan, and the time involved in investigating and decision-making on exactly what is now required, with possible appeals, could disrupt the professional's ability to provide what the child requires and disrupt the child's progress. A plan must allow professionals sufficient freedom to use their judgment on what to do in the circumstances as they are at the time. A Tribunal is entitled to use its expertise to decide on the proper balance between precision and flexibility: *BB v Barnet London Borough Council* [2019] UKUT 285 (AAC) at [23].

Provision should normally be quantified (see the Code of Practice at paragraph 9.69), but there is no absolute and universal requirement that provision should be quantified in terms of hours per week: *L v Clarke and Somerset* [1998] ELR 129 at [25].

Examples of words or phrases which, without further specification, may well give rise to problems include: 'regular', 'periodic', 'frequent', 'as appropriate', 'as required', 'as advised', 'subject to review', 'small classes', 'small groups', 'support', 'opportunities for', 'access to', 'a programme devised by', 'a programme to develop', 'initially… thereafter…', 'specialist', and 'the equivalent of [X] hours of support'. It is arguable that an EHC plan may state the arrangements for funding the provision, but that does not affect the legal requirement to specify the provision itself in Section F.

In *JD v South Tyneside* [2016] UKUT 9 (AAC) at [8], [10] and [13] Mitchell J held that provision in Part 3 of the statement prefaced by the words, 'it is recommended that' and, 'may be helpful' did not meet the required standard of specificity: a 'recommendation' leaves doubt as to what is required; in fact, it suggests that nothing at all is *required.*

Reference to further assessment or review in the future may give rise to problems. In *E v Rotherham MBC* [2002] ELR 266 at [31-32] Bell J held that specification of provision which left it open whether SALT provision would continue after a specified date was not permissible, where the child's speech and language needs were his primary needs and there was no good reason to believe that his need for SALT provision would be any less after the specified date. However, in *CL v Hampshire CC* [2011] UKUT 468 (AAC) at [16], a reference to an assessment that might take place in the future was held to be permissible. In *DM v Cornwall CC (SEN)* [2022] UKUT 230 (AAC) at [8-19], Wright J contrasted the termly reviews which the Tribunal had specified in that case, which were needed to review and progress the interventions which had been specified – which were permissible – with a review which might be specified in a plan which would allow for the provision in Section F to be fundamentally changed outside of the statutory review process, 'by the back door', with no mechanism for that change to be challenged – which would not be permissible.

Problems may arise if Section F specifies provision which can only be delivered by a specific person (individual or corporate). In *LB Redbridge v HO* (SENT) [2020] UKUT 323 the disputed provision was support "from a trusted and familiar psychologist". Lane J held at [23] and [27] that this provision was too vague in respect of content, impermissibly retrofitted to require, in practice, only one psychologist (the practical reality was that there was only one practitioner who would 'fit the bill'), contained selection criteria entirely subjective to the pupil, and might make compliance by the local authority a practical impossibility. There was no guarantee that the practitioner in question would accept the position or remain with it or remain 'trusted' in the subjective view of the child, and the LA would have no control, oversight of or right to objective assessment of the psychologist or the content and progress of the sessions. *DM v Cornwall CC (SEN)* [2022] UKUT 230 (AAC) was a case in which the plan named an individual to draft a part of the special educational provision to be made. Wright J held, at [27], that the problem here was that the individual was not a lawful delegate or proxy for the LA and the specification of provision in this way might carry a serious risk of the LA being in breach of its duty to secure the provision under section 42(2). A comparable issue arose in *JD v South Tyneside* [2016] UKUT 9 where section F of the EHC plan specified an occupational therapy programme *and* specified that it would be devised and implemented by the local NHS Foundation Trust, which, Mitchell J held, at [14], was not permissible as the Trust was under no duty to make the provision. Similarly, Section F must not specify provision which directly or indirectly imposes an obligation on parents or privately paid carers to provide it: *A v Cambridgeshire* [2002] EWHC 2391 at [60] and *TW and KW v Hampshire County Council* (SEN) [2022] UKUT 305 (AAC).

Where a special school is under consideration a lower degree of specificity *may* be appropriate in relation to any specification of what provision may require to be supplied by the school itself: *S v SENDIST* [2007] EWHC 1139 at [36]. In an appropriate case, the fact that provision is being made at a special school or college *may* permit more flexibility than when a mainstream school is involved: *East Sussex CC v TW* [2016] UKUT 528 (AAC) at [41]. In *E v Newham LBC* [2003] ELR 286 at [65] the Court of Appeal stated the factors specific to that case which weighed with them, which included that parents had wanted a mainstream school to be specified, and in that context greater specificity might well be appropriate because staff had to be brought in, whereas in the context of a special school such staff were in principle available, however the parents had reconciled themselves to the fact that a special school rather than a mainstream school was, for the time being, appropriate.

In *Worcestershire CC v SE* [2020] UKUT 217 (AAC) at [74] West J undertook a review of the case law on 'specificity' and set out a summary of the principles which could be 'distilled' from it.

Powers of the First-tier Tribunal in 'Section F' appeals, and compliance

By regulation 43(1) of the 2014 Regulations, before determining any appeal, the First-tier Tribunal may, with the agreement of the parties, correct any deficiencies in the EHC Plan which relate to the SEN or special educational provision for the child or the young person.

By regulation 43(2)(a) and (f), when determining a 'Section F' appeal, the powers of First-tier Tribunal include the power to dismiss the appeal, or to order the local authority to continue to maintain the EHC Plan with amendments so far as that relates to the special educational provision in the plan. The Tribunal also has a power to make "any other consequential amendments as [it] thinks fit": regulation 43(2)(f). In *S v Worcestershire CC (SEN)* [2017] UKUT 0092 (AAC) at [84-85] the Upper Tribunal held that this meant the Tribunal could make consequential amendments to the outcomes stated in Section E.

By regulation 44(2)(e), where the order requires the local authority to amend the special educational provision specified in an EHC Plan, the LA must issue the amended EHC Plan within 5 weeks of the order being made. As for the timeframe within which the provision must be put in place, see *BA v Nottinghamshire CC* [2021] EWHC 1348 (Admin) at [37]. Where the order requires the LA to continue to maintain an EHC Plan in its existing form, the LA must continue to maintain the EHC Plan (regulation 44(2)(g)). Regulation 44(2) is subject any direction made by the First-tier Tribunal: regulation 44(1).

In an unopposed appeal, by regulation 45 the Tribunal is not required to make an order. If the appeal is made under section 51(2)(c)(ii) or (e) of the 2014 Act, the local authority must issue the amended EHC plan to those specified in regulation 22(3) within 5 weeks of the date it notifies the First-tier Tribunal that it will not oppose the appeal before it submits a response: regulation 45(4).

CHAPTER SIX

'SECTION I' APPEALS

Overview

Sections 33, 38 and 39 of the Children and Families Act 2014, and regulation 12(1)(i) of the Special Educational Needs and Disability Regulations 2014, as well as section 9 of the Education Act 1996, are the key provisions which govern Section I of EHC plans.

By subsections 51(1) and 51(2)(c) 2014 Act Part 3, where an EHC plan is maintained for the child or young person, the child's parent or the young person may appeal to the First-tier Tribunal against the school or other institution named in the plan, or the type of school or other institution specified in the plan (subsection 51(2)(c)(iii)) or, if no school or other institution is named in the plan, that fact (subsection 51(2)(c)(iv)). By subsection 51(2(e), the child's parent or the young person may appeal against a decision of a local authority not to secure the amendment or replacement of an EHC plan it maintains for the child or young person following a review or re-assessment under section 44. By subsection 51(3), the circumstances in which a parent or young person may bring an appeal under subsection 51(2(c) are when an EHC plan is first finalised (s. 51(3)(a)) and following an amendment or replacement of the plan (s. 51(3)(b)). Regulations 18 to 28 of the 2014 Regulations deal with reviewing, re-assessing, amending and replacing EHC plans.

Section 38 of the 2014 Act Part 3 requires a local authority, where it is required to secure that an EHC plan is prepared for a child or young person, to send a *draft* of the EHC plan to the child's parent or the young person (s. 38(2)(a)), which must *not* name a school or other institution or specify a type of school or other institution (s. 38(5)).

The local authority must *also* give the parent or young person notice of his or her right, *inter alia,* to request the authority to secure that a particular school or other institution within subsection 38(3) is named in the plan (s. 38(2)(b)(ii)). The notice must specify a period before the end of which any request must be made (s. 38(4)); by regulation 13 of the 2014 Regulations, this must be at least 15 days, beginning with the day on which the draft plan was served.

A school or other institution is within subsection 38(3) if it is (a) a maintained school; (b) a maintained nursery school; (c) an Academy; (d) an institution within the further education sector in England; (e) a non-maintained special school; (f) an institution approved by the Secretary of State under section 41 (independent special schools and special post-16 institutions: approval). An explanation of these types of school or other institution is provided in this Chapter, below.

If, before the end of the period specified in the notice, a request is made to the local authority under section 38(2)(b) to secure that a particular school or other institution within subsection 38(3) is named in the plan, the LA must first consult the governing body, proprietor or principal of the school or other institution, the governing body, proprietor or principal of any other school or other institution the authority is considering having named in the plan, and if such school or other institution is maintained by another local authority, that authority: section 39(2). The school or other institution should respond within 15 days: SEND Code of Practice paragraph 9.83. This 'consultation response' is likely to form a key part of the evidence in any 'Section I' appeal.

Then, by section 39(3), the local authority <u>must</u> secure that the EHC plan names the school or other institution specified in the request <u>unless</u> subsection 39(4) applies.

Subsection 39(4) applies in three situations. The first situation is where the school or other institution requested is unsuitable for the age, ability, aptitude or special educational needs of the child or young person concerned (subsection 39(4)(a)). The second situation is where the attendance of the child or young person at the requested school or other institution would be incompatible with the provision of efficient education for others (subsection 39(4)(b)(i)). The third situation is where the attendance of the child or young person at the requested school or other institution would be incompatible with the efficient use of resources (subsection 39(4)(b)(ii)). These three types of situations are explained further in this Chapter, below.

Where any of these situations specified in subsection 39(4) apply, the local authority must secure that the plan *names* a school or other institution which the LA thinks would be appropriate for the child or young person or specifies the *type* of school or other institution which the LA thinks would be appropriate for the child or young person: subsection 39(5). Consequently, in a 'Section I' appeal, where the appellant has requested a school or other institution within subsection 38(3), the First-tier Tribunal, 'standing in the shoes' of the LA, must name the school or other institution requested by the appellant unless any of the three situations specified in subsection 39(4) apply.

If one or more of the three types of situations specified in subsection 39(4) do apply, then the local authority, and the First-tier Tribunal, 'standing in the shoes' of the LA, must secure that the plan *names* a school or other institution which the LA thinks would be "appropriate" for the child or young person, or specifies the *type* of school or other institution which the local authority thinks would be "appropriate" for the child or young person: subsection 39(5). By section 33, that "appropriate" school or other institution, or type of school or other institution must be a maintained nursery school, mainstream school or mainstream post-16 institution, unless certain conditions specified in section 33 apply. What this all means is explained further in this Chapter, below.

Before securing that the EHC plan names a school or other institution in these circumstances, the local authority must (if it has not already done so) consult the governing body, proprietor or principal of any school or other institution the authority is considering having named in the plan, and if that school or other institution is maintained by another local authority, that authority.

The consequence of the local authority (or, in the context of an appeal, the First-tier Tribunal) naming a school or other institution in section I which is within subsection 38(3) is that the governing body, proprietor or principal of the school or other institution must admit the child or young person for whom the plan is maintained. This is the 'duty to admit' under section 43 of the 2013 Act. The 'duty to admit' has effect regardless of any duty imposed on the governing body of a school by section 1(6) of Schools Standards and Framework Act 1998 (which relates to the limit imposed by the Secretary of State on class sizes for infant classes at maintained schools) but does not affect any power subsequently to exclude the pupil or student from the school or other institution (subsections 43(3); 43(4)).

Children with EHC plans can attend more than one school under a dual placement. There is some guidance on this in the 2015 Code of Practice at paragraphs 9.85-9.86.

A child's parent or young person may also make representations for a place at a particular school or other institution which is not within subsection 38(3). This situation, and the operation of section 9 in 'Section I appeals' is explained further in this Chapter, below.

The special situation provided for by section 61 of the 2014 Act, whereby special educational provision may be made otherwise than in a school or post-16 institution or a place at which relevant early years education is provided, sometimes referred to by the shorthand 'EOTAS', is addressed in Chapter 7.

The schools and other institutions falling within subsection 38(3) of the Children and Families Act 2014 Part 3

A maintained school for the purposes of section 38(3)(a) means a community, foundation or voluntary school within the meaning of School Standards and Framework Act 1998, or a community or foundation special school (within the meaning of the 1999 Act) not established in a hospital: section 83 of the 2014 Act. A community or foundation special school will be a "special school" if it is specially organised to make special educational provision for pupils with special educational needs: section 337 of the Education Act 1996.

<u>A maintained nursery school</u> for the purposes of section 38(3)(b) has the meaning given by section 22(9) of the School Standards and Framework Act 1998: section 579 of the 1996 Act.

<u>An Academy</u> for the purposes of section 38(3(c) means an educational institution to which Academy arrangements relate; "Academy arrangements" has the meaning given by section 1 of the Academies Act 2010: section 579 of the 1996 Act.

As for the meaning of an "<u>institution within the further education sector in England</u>" for the purposes of section 38(3)(d), the starting point is section 91 of the Further and Higher Education Act 1992 which applies for the interpretation of the Education Acts. References to institutions within the further education sector are to institutions conducted by further education corporations, to designated institutions for the purposes of Part I of the 1992 Act (defined in section 28(4)), and to sixth form colleges. "Further education corporation" is defined by section 17 of the 1992 Act. Sixth form colleges are institutions conducted by sixth form college corporations: section 91(3A) of the 1992 Act. Sections 33A-C of the 1992 Act make provision for the Secretary of State to designate or establish, by order, bodies corporate into sixth form college corporations.

A "<u>non-maintained special school</u>" for the purposes of section 38(3)(e) is explained with reference to sections 342 and 337A of the 1996 Act. By section 342 the Secretary of State may approve any school in England which is specially organised to make special educational provision for pupils with special educational needs and is not a community or foundation special school or an Academy school. A 'non-maintained special school means a school that is approved under that section: section 337A. These schools are subject to the Non-Maintained Special Schools (England) Regulations 2015 (SI 2015/728) and may not be conducted for profit.

A "institution approved by the Secretary of State under section 41 (independent special schools and special post-16 institutions: approval)" for the purposes of section 38(3)(f)) is explained with reference to section 41 of the 2014 Act. Under section 41, the Secretary of State may approve an institution within subsection 41(2) for the purpose of enabling the institution to be the subject of a request for it to be named in an EHC plan. An institution in England is within subsection 41(2) if it is an independent educational institution within the meaning of Chapter 1 of Part 4 of the Education and Skills Act 2008 which has been entered on the register of independent educational institutions in England (kept under section 95 of that Act) and which is specially organised to make special educational provision for students with special educational needs, or it is a special post-16 institution which is not an institution within the further education sector or a 16 to 19 Academy. Part 5 of the 2014 Regulations makes further provision in relation to Independent Special Schools and Special Post-16 Institutions approved under section 41. By regulation 62, the Secretary of State must publish a list of all institutions that have been approved, and have not had that approval withdrawn, on the Internet.

Lists of non-maintained special schools and institutions approved under section 41 can be found on the gov.uk website.

Where parents or a young person request a school or institution which does not fall within subsection 38(3) of the 2014 Act

Section I can name a school or institution which does not fall within subsection 38(3) of the 2014 Act: *S v Worcestershire CC* (SEN) [2017] UKUT 92 (AAC) at [75] and [88] and *LB Hillingdon v SS and others (SEN)* [2017] UKUT 250 (AAC); [2019] AACR 9 at [43-57].

S v Worcestershire concerned a young person who was a 'pupil' for the purposes of sections 3 and 9 of the 1996 Act who wanted to attend a school which did not fall within subsection 38(3) of the 2014 Act. Mitchell J held, at [75] and [88], that the section 39 'presumption' in favour of a young person's preferred placement does not apply where he seeks an independent school that is not approved under section 41, and consequently section 40(2) required the Tribunal to specify the institution or type of institution it considered "appropriate". He added that where the terms of section 9 of the Education Act 1996 apply, the Tribunal must also act in accordance with the requirements of that section (see the summary of the law in *Hammersmith & Fulham LBC v L* [2015] UKUT 0523 (AAC)). The provisions of section 9 of the 1996 Act are considered further in this Chapter, below.

LB Hillingdon v SS and others (SEN) 2017] UKUT 250 (AAC); [2019] AACR 9 concerned a young person who was not a pupil for the purposes of sections 3 and 9 of the 1996 Act who wanted to attend an institution which did not fall within subsection 38(3) of the 2014 Act. Ward J confirmed, at [43-57], that the Tribunal had a power to name that institution in Section I which did not derive from section 9 of the 1996 Act. Section 9 is not a power-giving provision: rather, it goes to whether an ability to express a preference arises, and, if it does, to what weight should be given to that preference. Section 38 of the 2014 Act concerns the process under which a preference for a particular school or institution may be expressed and receive a degree of statutory support, but does not limit the range of schools and institutions which may be named in an EHC plan albeit a preference for those not within section 38(3) will not receive that statutory support. Consequently, an independent school which does not fall within subsection 38(3) can be named under section 40(2) and the test is simply 'appropriateness'.

Section 9 of the Education Act 1996

Section 9 of the 1996 Act reads as follows:

> *"In exercising or performing all their respective powers and duties under the Education Acts, the Secretary of State and local authorities shall have regard to the general principle that pupils are to be educated in accordance with the wishes of their parents, so far as that is compatible with the provision of efficient instruction and training and the avoidance of unreasonable public expenditure."*

As observed by Mitchell J in *Hammersmith & Fulham LBC v L & F* [2015] UKUT 523 (AAC) at [39], section 9 can be traced back to the Education Act 1944 and a body of authorities has developed.

Section 9 applies expressly to a local authority's power *and* duties which are those under the "Education Acts" which are listed in section 578(1) of the 1996 Act. These include the 1996 Act and now include Part 3 (and section 100) of the 2014 Act. Thus, it operates in a wide range of statutory contexts.

"Public expenditure" for the purposes of section 9 means expenditure incurred by *any* public body; it is not limited to expenditure by the local authority in the exercise of its education functions: *WH v Warrington BC* [2014] EWCA Civ 398 at [27]. In that case the local authority named a maintained day special school in the child's statement but also provided residential respite care. The parent wanted the child to attend an independent residential special school and argued that the cost comparison for the purpose of section 9 should include the cost of respite care.

Where the wishes of the parent are for their child to attend a particular school, the application of section 9 may call for findings to be made as to the 'additional' costs for the local authority and any other public authority of the rival schools and, if the school of parental choice costs more, an exercise of judgment in deciding whether, on the costs identified, a placement at that school would involve unreasonable expenditure. When conducting the 'balancing exercise', the Tribunal is obliged to take account of wider social and health benefits when deciding whether additional public expenditure is unreasonable: *K v LB Hillingdon* [2011] AACR 31; [2011] UKUT 71 at [29]; *London Borough of Croydon v K-A* [2022] UKUT 106 (AAC).

The application of section 9 may also call for findings and a judgment to be made as to whether placement at that school would be 'compatible' with 'the provision of efficient instruction and training'. In *R (Hampshire CC) v R* [2009] EWHC 626 Stadlen J held, at [37] with reference to the Council's arguments at [28], that the words, "provision of efficient instruction and training" are entirely general and at large and unlimited: they do not relate solely to the instruction and training of the pupil whose parents' wishes are in issue, nor do they relate solely to the instruction and training of the children or young people with whom that pupil would be educated.

A parental preference is not determinative, even if it is compatible with the provision of efficient instruction and training and the avoidance of unreasonable public expenditure. In *Watt v Kesteven County Council* [1955] 1 QB 408 at [424] Denning LJ said, "[Section 9] does not say that pupils must in all cases be educated in accordance with the wishes of their parents. It only lays down a general principle to which the county council must have regard. This leads it open to the county council to have regard to other things as well, and also to make exceptions to the general principle if it thinks fit to do so." Lord Slyn, giving the judgment of the House of Lords in *B v Harrow London Borough* Council (No. 1) [2000] 1 WLR 223 at [229H], made the same point, albeit probably *obiter*: "I do not consider that section 9 of the Act means that parental preference is to prevail unless it involves unreasonable public expenditure".

However, as Mitchell J observed in *Hammersmith & Fulham LBC v L & F* [2015] UKUT 523 (AAC) at [40], cases tend to be argued before the First-tier Tribunal on the basis that if there is no unreasonable expenditure, effect will be given to parental preference.

This is reflected in the way that the Upper Tribunal (Levenson J) at [9] in *IM v LB Croydon* [2010] UKUT 205 (AAC) framed the questions to be decided in a case in which needs have been identified and in which the LEA and the parents each wish a different school to be named, and in which the First-tier Tribunal has to choose between the two schools. The questions are (a) "Are both schools appropriate to meet the need? A school that is not appropriate cannot be named." (b) "If they are both appropriate, which is the school preferred by the parents? Unless (c) applies, that school must be named." (c) "Would naming the school preferred by parents be incompatible with the provision of efficient instruction and training or the avoidance of unreasonable public expenditure? If so the school suggested by the local education authority must be named."

However, the High Court held in *Hampshire v R & SENDIST* [2009] EWHC 626, at [65], that even if the Tribunal finds 'incompatibility' under section 9, that does not entitle it to ignore the reasons lying behind the parents' choice of school. Those are matters still to be taken into account by the Tribunal in the exercise of its discretion and weighed in the balance among the other factors which the Tribunal considers are relevant.

In addition, the Court of Appeal held in *Richardson v Solihull* [1998] EWCA Civ 3535 at [51] that the Tribunal is not obliged to name the school requested by the parent even if that is capable of meeting the child's SEN and the school named by the LEA is found not to be appropriate. The Tribunal must exercise its own judgment and have regard to the duty on the LEA to avoid unreasonable public expenditure and to use resources efficiently; "It defies common sense that even though the school named by the parent is a considerably more expensive residential school and even though the SENT regards that school as providing far more than needed, the SENT has no choice but to require the naming of the school of the parent's choice." In such circumstances the Tribunal has a choice: it can adjourn the hearing to enable the LEA to come up with the name of another school capable of delivering the special educational provision, or it can determine the appeal by naming no school. This assumes that the special educational provision has been described satisfactorily. If it has not, then it can amend the description.

Section 9 expressly applies to the situation of "pupils", defined in the 1996 Act at section 3. This definition excludes many young people for whom EHC plans are maintained under the 2014 Act Part 3. However, as noted above, in *LB Hillingdon v SS and others (SEN)* [2019] AACR 9 the Upper Tribunal confirmed that Section I can name an institution which does not fall within section 38(3) of the 2014 Act even where section 9 of the 1996 Act does not apply, and the test is simply 'appropriateness' under section 40(2) of the 2014 Act.

In summary, a child's parent or a young person may request a place at a particular school or other institution which is <u>not</u> within subsection 38(3) and the local authority must specify a name or type of school or institution in Section I under section 40(2), having considered the request under the provisions of section 9 of the 1996 Act if that applies. Under section 9, the First-tier Tribunal will usually give effect to the parental preference if it would not involve unreasonable public expenditure. It is less usual for local authorities to oppose parental preference on grounds of incompatibility with the provision of efficient instruction and training. Where a child's parent or a young person requests a school or other institution which <u>is</u> within subsection 38(3), the Tribunal, 'standing in the shoes' of the local authority, <u>must</u> name the school or other institution requested by the appellant <u>unless</u> any of the three situations specified in subsection 39(4) of the 2014 Act apply. The Tribunal 'standing in the shoes' of the LA, must *also* apply the principle stated in section 9 of the 1996 where the child or young person is a pupil and section 9 applies: *O v Lewisham* [2007] EWHC 2130 at [16] and *Ealing v SENDIST & K* [2008] EWHC 193 (Admin).

The case law on how to assess 'expenditure' for the purposes of the comparison under section 9 is considered further in this Chapter, below.

The three types of situations specified in subsection 39(4) of the 2014 Act

<u>Where the school or other institution requested is unsuitable for the age, ability, aptitude or special educational needs of the child or young person concerned (subsection 39(4)(a))</u>

In *A J v. London Borough of Croydon* [2020] UKUT 246 (AAC) the Upper Tribunal held (at [137] that First-tier Tribunal had made an error of law by placing a burden of proof onto the appellant parents to show that their preferred placement was suitable.

Even where a local authority does not oppose a 'Section I' appeal on the 'suitability' ground, the Tribunal, exercising its inquisitorial powers, may be expected to take steps to satisfy itself that the school or other institution requested is suitable for the age, ability, aptitude or special educational needs of the child or young person concerned. Case management directions in 'Section I' appeals will usually direct the parties to provide a copy of the most recent Ofsted report and prospectus/brochure for the school or institution they propose to name in Section I.

A school is not necessarily "unsuitable" for the purposes of section 39(4)(a) – or not "appropriate" for the purposes of section 39(5) – simply because it does not have the necessary facilities in place at the date of the hearing. The fact that the provision is specified on the basis of a promise or assurance as to the future rather than existing fact is not, as a matter of law, something which prohibits the Tribunal from specifying that provision: *R (L) v London Borough of Southwark* [2005] EWHC 1210 at [14]. If the Tribunal names the school in circumstances where there is no acceptable evidence that the provision will be available, the Tribunal will have acted irrationally, but it is for the Tribunal to assess the assurances put before it by, in that case, the local education authority, and the matters put before it by both parties, with a view to determining whether it can prudently and safely rely on the promise or assurance made: at [13].

A school may not be 'unsuitable' even if it has no space available at all. In *Hampshire County Council v JP* [2009] UKUT 239 (AAC) parents sought a residential placement at a school, 'PV', which did not have a place available. The Tribunal specified a placement on a day basis first at 'O' School, proposed by the local authority, "and then once a 52-week placement at [PV] is available on a residential basis for fifty-two weeks a year at [PV] School." The Upper Tribunal held, at [21-22], that the First-tier Tribunal had not erred in law in specifying a placement at PV School merely because there was a risk that a place would not be available for nine months. The Tribunal had considered there to be a substantial likelihood of a place becoming available then. Moreover, the parent herself had judged that waiting for a place at PV School was preferable to continuing the search elsewhere. Once the Tribunal had accepted the child's need for a placement in a residential school, it was entitled to consider that this was the best that could be achieved for the child.

However, the Upper Tribunal stated, at [22], there were substantial arguments to be made against the First-tier Tribunal's approach. The local authority suspected that the decision of the First-tier Tribunal in fact contributed to the subsequent breakdown of the child's placement at O school. Moreover, a willingness to risk his having to remain at O school for as long as nine months raises the question as to whether it really was unsuitable for him and whether the advantages to him of going to PV School really justified the extra expenditure that there would be.

Where the attendance of the child or young person at the requested school or other institution would be incompatible with the provision of efficient education for others (subsection 39(4)(b)(i))

By paragraph 3(3) of Schedule 27 of the 1996 Act (the statutory 'predecessor' to subsection 39(4) of the 2014 Act) the local authority had to specify the name of the school requested by the parent under paragraph 3(1) unless "the attendance of the child at the school would be incompatible with the provision of efficient education for the children with whom he would be educated or the efficient use of resources". This was considered by Mesher J in *NA v London Borough of Barnet* [2010] UKUT 180 (AAC) at [32-36].

Mesher J considered the statement of Gibbs J in *Essex County Council v SENDIST and S* [2006] ELR 452 at paragraph [29], that the word `incompatible' is a strong term, with a suggestion that it has a stronger meaning than "prejudicial to". Essentially the same point was made in *Hampshire* CC v R and SENDIST [2009] EWHC 626 at [56]: the question is not whether the child's attendance at that school "would have an impact on the efficiency of the education of those children, but whether that impact is so great that his attendance would be incompatible with the efficiency of their education." Mesher J agreed that it was not enough for the purposes of paragraph 3(3)(b) of Schedule 27 of the 1996 Act that the quality of education provided for other children would be reduced from the very highest standard to something a little lower, nor did it have to be shown that no meaningful education at all would be provided for some other child or that the admission of the child in question would tip the school into failure: at [33-34]. "Efficient education" indicates a standard, not the very highest desirable standard or the very basic minimum, but something in between that, which the members of the First-tier Tribunal are uniquely qualified by their expertise and experience to recognise in particular cases. Although "incompatible" is indeed a very strong word, indicating that there is no way of avoiding the admission of the single child involved reducing the quality of education provided to some other children with whom he would be educated below that standard, its force must be applied in the context of that standard: at [34]. Mesher J did not think that the Upper Tribunal should go any further in attempting to define the standards embodied in "efficient education" but drew attention to the guidance in paragraph 40 of the *Inclusive Schooling* document that it meant, "providing for each child a suitable and appropriate education in terms of a child's age, ability, aptitude and any special educational needs he/she may have": at [35]. Depending on the circumstances of particular cases, it will often be necessary for a Tribunal to identify just what difference it finds that the admission of the single child would make before it can go on to make the judgment about whether the degree of impact the child's attendance would have would meet the 'incompatibility' test: at [37].

Paragraph 3(3) of schedule 27 of the 1996 Act referred to the provision of efficient education "for the children with whom [the child] would be educated" and Mesher J held, at [37], that this must be applied by reference to the circumstances only of the child in question and other children who are already known or predicted to be in the category of those who would be educated with the child: although the overall context of the school would be relevant, especially in relation to whether adjustments could be made elsewhere to avoid an incompatibility that would other otherwise arise, the circumstances of other children who might possibly be admitted, particularly as the result of other outstanding appeals, could not be taken into account. Subsection 39(4)(b)(i) of the 2014 Act, however, simply refers to the provision of efficient education "for others".

Where the attendance of the child or young person at the requested school or other institution would be incompatible with the efficient use of resources (subsection 39(4)(b)(ii))

What resources?

It seems relatively clear from the case law that, for the purpose of subsection 39(4)(ii) of the 2014 Act, the resources in question are those of the local authority who is responsible for the child or young person for the purposes of the 2014 Act Part 3. In *PD and AD v Stockton-on-Tees BC* (SEN) [2019] UKUT 57 (AAC) at [48] Lane J stated, "It has long been decided in both the courts and Upper Tribunal that the tests under the old Schedule 27 paragraph 3(3) (which has now morphed into section 39(4) and section 9 are different. It is not necessary to extend the length of this decision by a detailed exposition of the well-known case law since the facts of this appeal admit of only one answer. It is enough to say that section 39(4) requires the LA or the Tribunal standing in its shoes to look at the resources of the LA itself whereas section 9 requires the Tribunal to take a 'holistic' look and take a wide view of public expenditure rather than just the resources of the LA."

In *B v Harrow London Borough Council (No. 1)* [2000] 1 WLR 223, the choice was between two maintained special schools: one maintained by Harrow LBC, the other maintained by a neighbouring authority, Hillingdon. If the child attended the Hillingdon school, provision would be made by Hillingdon LBC and Harrow LBC would pay a sum to Hillingdon LBC pursuant to regulation 3 of the Education (Inter-authority Recoupment) Regulations 1994. However, there would be an unfilled vacancy at the Harrow school which Harrow LBC would also have to fund (under the schools' funding arrangements in place at the relevant time, special schools' funding was geared to the number of pupils for whom it was anticipated the school would need to provide places). Consequently, there would be no cost to Hillingdon but there would be a 'double' cost to Harrow. The House of Lords concluded (per Lord Slynn at p 229A, 229H) that the resources in question were the those of the local education authority which was "responsible" for the child because the child was "in their area" per section 321(3) of the 1996 Act.

In *WH v Warrington Borough Council* [2014] EWCA Civ 398*)*, a case on the interpretation of "public expenditure" for the purposes of section 9 of the 1996 Act, the Court of Appeal, at [27], contrasted the language used in section 9, where the word "public" is used, with the language of Schedule 27 paragraph 3(3) of the 1996 Act, where the word "public" was not used.

However, it may be argued that that the law is not settled as to whether the resources in question are the resources the local authority has for the discharge of its education functions or any of its functions. In *WH v Warrington Borough Council*, the "public" expenditure in question would have been from the resources of the same local authority, providing respite care for the child. It may also be argued that there is some inconsistency in the case law, in that in *PM v Worcestershire County Council* [2022] UKUT 53 (AAC) the Upper Tribunal, at 44(d), took funding from the Education and Skills Funding Agency into account for the purposes of determining whether a placement would be 'incompatible with the efficient use of resources' under section 39(4). However, it was not argued in that case that ESFA funding did not fall within the 'resources' in question.

Specific provisions of the Schools Standards and Framework Act 1998 indicate that payments made by a local authority to a maintained school under delegated arrangements are to be treated as the resources of the local authority. These provisions were considered in *X City Council v SENDIST, AB, MB & GB* [2007] EWHC 2278 in which Underhill J held, at [12-13], that Sedley LJ in *Oxfordshire County Council v GB & Others* [2001] EWCA Civ, in referring at [15-17] to "the LEA's annual budget", plainly did not have in mind a distinction between payment by the LEA directly from its own pocket and payment by the school under delegated arrangements. That conclusion, which seemed right to Underhill J as a matter of principle, was reinforced by the terms of subsection 49(5) of the 1998 Act: "Any amount made available by a local education authority to the governing body of a maintained school (whether under section 50 or otherwise) (a) shall remain the property of the authority until spent by the governing body or the head teacher; and (b) when spent by the governing body or the head teacher, shall be taken to be spent by them or him as the authority's agent". Underhill J held that subsection 49(5) shows that, notwithstanding the power given to the school to spend the money under the delegated arrangements, the expenditure remains ultimately that of the Council.

'Incompatibility'

In *Essex County Council v SENDIST* [2006] EWHC 1105 (Admin) at [24] to [32] the High Court held that the words, 'incompatible with the efficient use of resources' meant, will the extra expense in fulfilling parental wishes be so high as to be incompatible with the efficient use of the LEA's resources? It summarised that proposition as, will it be 'disproportionate'? It held that the LEA or the Tribunal, in the case of an appeal, must carry out a balancing exercise, weighing "the amount of resources involved in maintaining the child at a particular school, the relative merits of possible schools for the child and a broad range of relevant educational factors": at [31].

As for how to calculate the <u>amount</u> of resources involved in maintaining a child or young person at a particular school or institution, there is a body of case law which provides some guidance. Some of it arises from appeals where section 9 of the 1996 Act was in play. This case law is considered in the section below.

Assessing the amount of 'resources' or 'public expenditure'

It may be material to consider the cost of the 'rival' placements over more than one year. In *Southampton v G* [2002] EWHC 1516, the school of parental choice prepared children for GCSE over a six-year rather than a five-year period. However, the Tribunal determined the appeal on the basis of the difference in annual costs and did not take into account the fact that the Council would have to pay for an additional year's costs should the school of parental choice be specified. The High Court held, at [20], that this was a material factor which the Tribunal had overlooked; this was a finely balanced case which turned on the cost of provision and it followed that the Tribunal's decision had to be quashed.

The Upper Tribunal, and the High Court before it, have declined to indicate any specific sum or threshold of additional expenditure that would in all cases constitute an inefficient use of resources or unreasonable public expenditure.

It may not be necessary to perform a precise calculation of the cost of maintaining the child or young person at the school or other institution in question. In *Slough Borough Council v Special Educational Needs and Disability Tribunal and Others [2010] EWCA Civ 668* Sedley LJ held, at [12-13], that it was legitimate for the Tribunal to have taken a 'short cut' when it found, as it did, that whatever the notional per capita cost of the maintained school was, it must exceed the £10,000 cost of the school of parental choice, with which it fell to be compared.

The cost involved in home to school transport

In *Birmingham City Council v KF* [2018] UKUT 261, Levenson J held at [19] that home to school transport is capable of being special educational provision *if* it educates or trains the child or young person as per subsection 21(5) of the 2014 Act. Where that applied, the local authority would have a duty to secure the transport under section 42 of the 2014 Act.

Except where subsection 21(5) applies, a local authority's duties to arrange home to school (or home to college) transport are set out in Part IX Chapter II of the 1996 Act, which deals with ancillary functions of local authorities. The provisions relating to transport in that Chapter are detailed, and an explanation of them lies outside the scope of this book. What follows is a very brief summary: the provisions relate to travel arrangements: (1) for "eligible" children which local authorities *must* make; (2) for children who are not "eligible" children which local authorities *may* make; (3) for young people of sixth form age (a category which includes young people with EHC plans up to age 25 where they are continuing on a course started before their 19th birthday); (4) for adults and young adults with EHC plans; and (5) for children receiving nursery education (early years education) otherwise than at school. The Department for Education's Home to School Travel and Transport

Statutory Guidance, July 2014, provides guidance on (1) and (2). The Department for Education's Post-16 Transport and Travel Support to Education and Training Statutory Guidance, January 2019, provides guidance on (3) and (4).

It follows that under the provisions of Part IX Chapter II of the 1996 Act, a local authority may have a power or a duty to pay for home to school or home to college transport. In *Staffordshire County Council* [2016] UKUT 246 (AAC) Lane J held, at [36], that the LA had a duty to make travel arrangements for the young person in question under section 508F of the 1996 Act *if* the LA considered that to be necessary having regard to all of the relevant circumstances, but this was not a 'pure discretion': "although the question of what is necessary is a matter for them, in deciding that question they must exercise their judgment judiciously and in good faith. If they come to the conclusion that it is necessary, they must make the necessary arrangements and the transportation must be free of charge."

In *Oxfordshire County Council v GB & Others* [2001] EWCA Civ 1358 Sedley LJ held, at [16-18], that the costs comparison will include comparative 'on-costs' which may or may not include home to school transport. In that case, the taxi that would transport the child was already being used to carry two children to the school, and to add the child to its passengers would cost the LEA no more.

In *Dudley MBC v JS* [2012] EWCA Civ 346 the Court of Appeal held, at [47], that the first stage is to consider the additional travel costs that would be incurred if the parents' preferred school were to be named and the local authority came under a duty under section 508B of the 1996 Act to fund travel arrangements. If the Tribunal concludes that the additional cost is *not* incompatible with the efficient use of resources (or that any *prima facie* incompatibility is outweighed by the educational and other advantages to the child of attending the parents' preferred school) then the the parents' preferred school must be named. If the Tribunal concludes that there *would* be an incompatibility with the efficient use of resources for the LA to meet the additional transport costs to the parent's preferred school, then there is no requirement to specify the latter. The

Tribunal should also consider whether that school should be specified taking account of the duty to have regard to parental preference under section 9 and applying the potentially broader calculus of "unreasonable public expenditure". However, section 9 of the Act does *not* mean that parental preference is to prevail unless it involves unreasonable public expenditure.

Parents may offer to take responsibility for the costs of transport to and from their preferred school which would reduce the 'comparative cost' of that school. The Court of Appeal held in *Dudley MBC v JS* [2012] EWCA Civ 346 at [47] that if the parents' preferred school should be named at the *first* stage of enquiry, under either statutory basis, then the LA would *not* be allowed to put a condition on the child's attendance at that school, that the parents be responsible for transport, with the nearer school specified if that condition were not met. However, if the parents' preferred school were *not* named at the first stage the Tribunal should go on to consider a further stage of enquiry, by asking whether, if the LA did *not* have to meet the additional transport costs, the parental preference could to that extent be accommodated without incompatibility with the efficient use of recourses. *R(M) v Sutton London Borough Council* [2007] EWCA Civ 790 is also authority that the parents' preferred school can be named on the condition that the parents take responsibility for the costs of transport to and from the school.

In *S v MR v Carmarthenshire CC* [2021] UKUT 294, which related to an appeal before the Welsh Tribunal, Jacobs J, at [14], summarised the line of authorities, including *Dudley MBC v JS*, which require a Tribunal, when undertaking a comparison of costs, to take into account any parental offer to take responsibility for transport costs. Jacobs J held, at [7], that the Tribunal had gone wrong in law by overlooking the possibility of naming more than one school in Part 4 of the statement of special educational needs and one school as the primary placement subject to the condition that the parents arrange transport at their own expense. Jacobs J held, at [13], that if parents could no longer take their son to school, there could be a statutory review of the statement, but it was permissible, indeed preferable, for the statement to provide for that contingency in advance. This works by naming two schools in Part 4.

The school preferred by parents is named on the express condition that parents arrange for transport at their own expense. Another school, usually the one proposed by the local authority, is also named in the event that the condition is no longer satisfied. The matter is dealt with as a condition on placement in Part 4; a formal written 'side agreement' between the parents and LA is unnecessary: at [16].

In *W v LB Hillingdon* [2005] EWHC 1580 Burnton J held, at [22], that if, for example, there is already a vehicle travelling between the vicinity of the child's address and X School with three children, and the cost of that transport is £20,000 a year, and there is no additional cost for taking a fourth child, the cost of the transport to X School for the purposes of the Tribunal's decision is zero; to take in such a case a quarter of the cost of the transport is an error. In that case it was also necessary for the Tribunal to consider whether an escort would be required for the child and, if so, what the cost of the escort would be and further, if an escort were required so that the child's journey to school involved *two* additional passengers, whether an additional vehicle would be required.

The cost involved in educating a pupil at an independent school

Section 63 of the 2014 Act ("Fees for special educational provision at non-maintained schools and post-16 institutions") requires a local authority, where a school, post-16 institution or place at which relevant early years education is named in the EHC plan, to pay any fees payable in respect of education or training provided for the child or young person at that setting in accordance with the EHC plan, including any fees in respect of the board and lodging (if special educational provision cannot be provided there unless the board and lodging are also provided).

Therefore, if a setting is non-maintained, it is the fee which would be payable by the local authority under section 63 which must be considered. Any additional fees the independent school or institution would charge for provision specified in section F of the EHC plan, such speech and language therapy, must also be taken into account.

In *Oxfordshire County Council v GB & Others* [2001] EWCA Civ 1358 Sedley LJ held at [16], that the cost of an independent school is assessed with reference to the annual fee, whatever the comparative capital costs or other sources of income of the establishment. If a fee is lower because of private or charitable funding, this will have no bearing on the quantum of public expenditure involved in a placement there.

As for whether parents (or a young person with means) can offer to pay a part of the fees of an independent school to reduce the 'additional' cost to the local authority or the 'public', the Court of Appeal gave this question substantial consideration in *Slough Borough Council v Special Educational Needs and Disability Tribunal & Others* [2010] EWCA Civ 668, but ultimately did not decide the issue. In that appeal, the LEA's case was that section 348 of the 1996 Act (the statutory predecessor to section 63) required it to pay the full fees of the school even though the school had voluntarily reduced its fees for that child in view of 'fundraising' for the school which the child's parents had undertaken. The parents argued that "the fees payable... for the child at the school" could only sensibly mean the fees the school was asking. Sedley LJ observed, at [16-18] and [21] that neither interpretation was without its problems and that the implications of the question were considerable.

The cost involved in educating a pupil at a maintained mainstream school

Chapter IV of the School Standards and Framework Act 1998 deals with the financing of maintained schools. Section 22 sets out the maintained schools which a particular local authority has a duty to maintain. The duty to maintain a school in this section includes the duty of "defraying all the expenses of maintaining it". By section 45, every maintained school has a "budget share" which represents a sum of money which is allocated to it by the authority which maintains it for every "funding period". Sections 49 and 50 make provision for a maintained school to have a "delegated budget" and for the LA to make available a sum equal to the school's budget share to be spent by the school's governing body which may spend this as they think fit for any purposes of the school (subsection 50(3)), subject to any provision "made by or under the scheme" – a reference to the scheme dealing with matters connected with the financing of schools, which, under section 48, every LA must have.

Regulations are made under the 1998 Act; currently these are the School and Early Years Finance (England) Regulations 2023/59 which came into force on 14 February 2023.

Oxfordshire County Council v GB & Others [2001] EWCA Civ 1358; *X City Council v SENDIST, AB, MB & GB* [2007] EWHC 2278; *Slough Borough Council v SENDT and Others* [2010] EWCA Civ 668; *EH v Kent CC* [2011] EWCA Civ 709 and *Hammersmith & Fulham LBC v L & F* [2015] UKUT 523 are a line of authorities in which the approach to costing the education of a pupil at a maintained mainstream school was considered.

In *Hammersmith,* Mitchell J noted, at [119-120], that it was a feature of the different funding regulations in force at the relevant time for all these decisions that a capitation fee would be paid to a maintained mainstream school by the LEA for each pupil placed there, referred to as the Age-Weighted Pupil Unit or 'AWPU'. Mitchell J analysed the features of the School and Early Years Finance (England) Regulations 2013 and noted that these provided for a specific minimum amount to be included in the school's budget share for each pupil for the coming funding period, once pupil numbers were identified: this was the 'current incarnation' of the 'AWPU'.

In *Hammersmith,* Michell J concluded, at [8] and [127-128], that where the choice is between an independent school and a maintained mainstream school without reserved places, the 'AWPU' normally represents an 'additional' cost for the purposes of the section 9 comparison, in accordance with *Kent.* Further, any additional funding required to meet the child's needs must also be taken into account, as required by *Kent* and *Oxfordshire.* If a local authority has some kind of dispensation from the normal requirements of the regulations or it has a financial scheme that deviates from the funding norm, it must bring this to the attention of the Tribunal and the other party, and the same applies if its per pupil funding for maintained mainstream schools is greater than the 'AWPU' minimum. That sum is to be taken as an 'additional' cost since it is 'money that follows the pupil'. The reasoning in *Hammersmith* is set out at [114-125]. The early authorities drew a distinction between 'AWPU' funding (school funding that was considered to be directly related to pupil numbers) and place funding (funding for a pre-determined number of places rather than by reference to pupil numbers). The starting point should be the legislative scheme for funding maintained schools: at [42]. Under the School and Early Years Finance (England) Regulations 2013, 'AWPU' funding was linked to pupil numbers rather than places: while some pupil numbers were to be ascertained some months before the start of the funding period, both dates fell within the same school year. It is likely that pupil transfers are concentrated in the gap between one school year ending and another beginning. 'AWPU' funding (including in its former guises) was not as closely related to actual pupil numbers as some of the earlier authorities assumed, but the differences between 'AWPU' funding and 'place funding' remained.

In *Hammersmith* Mitchell J also considered the operation of regulation 11(3) and Part 3 of the 2013 funding regulations and interpreted these to require a local authority to identify an amount within the budget share using the sum of £6,000 as the threshold below which the school would be expected to meet the additional costs of pupils at the school with SEN from its budget share. At [142] of *Hammersmith* Mitchell J declined to make a finding as to whether all or any costs under the regulation 11(3) £6,000 threshold (the 'notional SEN budget') were to be treated as an additional cost for section 9 purposes. It may be argued that following *P v Worcestershire CC* [2016] UKUT 120 (AAC) the law remains unclear in this regard.

In *Oxfordshire County Council v GB & Others* [2001] EWCA Civ 1358 Sedley LJ held, at [15], that 'unreasonable public expenditure' is not a legal term of art, but neither is it 'a protean concept capable of producing opposite outcomes on the same set of facts and figures depending on the individual tribunal's choice of accountancy method'. In that case it was not in dispute that the 'AWPU' cost should be included for the purpose of calculating the cost of educating the child at the maintained mainstream school in question, which had a hearing-impaired unit, because the 'AWPU' would be incurred only if the child went there. The dispute related to the Tribunal's decision to include the cost of home to school transport and the cost of 5 hours' provision from a Teacher for the Deaf who was on the staff of the hearing-impaired unit and would be paid the same regardless of whether the child joined the unit or not. Sedley LJ held that 'additional' or 'on-costs' come into account but, generally speaking, the 'existing' costs of providing the maintained school and of staffing it and its hearing-impaired unit do not come into account, although there may be particular cases in which some other method of comparison needs to be used: at [16-18].

In *X City Council v SENDIST, AB, MB & GB* [2007] EWHC 2278, Underhill J held, at [12-13], that any amount made available by a local education authority to the governing body of a maintained school under delegated arrangements was expenditure which was ultimately that of the Council (see further above).

In *EH v Kent CC* [2011] EWCA Civ 709 Sullivan LJ, at [25], rejected the argument that the "public expenditure" for the purposes of section 9 was the maintained school's expenditure of the budget allocated to it by the local authority, rather than the LA's budgetary allocation for the maintained school. Sullivan LJ held that there can be "public expenditure" for the purposes of section 9 at either or both stages of the process: when the LA allocates public funds to the school, and when the school spends those public funds. Sullivan LJ concluded, at [28-29] and [32], that the Tribunal should approach the question in a common-sense way. "Fancy accountancy footwork" which produces an unrealistic result, whether an excessive figure based on global costs including fixed costs, or a "cost free" placement, should not be persuasive. The LA's budgetary arrangements for an individual school, made in accordance with the 1998 Act and the applicable regulations, will usually be the sensible starting point.

The cost involved in educating a pupil at a maintained special school or maintained mainstream school with SEN-reserved places

In *Hammersmith & Fulham LBC v L & F* [2015] UKUT 523 (AAC) Mitchell J, at [7], gave guidance where the comparative cost analysis is between an independent school and a maintained special school or a maintained school with SEN-reserved places (a specialist unit). Generally, the analysis should proceed on the basis that where the special school or specialist unit has a vacancy, its place funding is not to be treated as an 'additional cost'. But, in line with the Court of Appeal's decisions in *Oxfordshire* and *Kent*, local authority 'top up' funding for the child's placement is an additional cost to be taken into account.

The reasoning in *Hammersmith* is at [114-125] of the decision. The early authorities drew a distinction between 'AWPU' funding (school funding that was considered to be directly related to pupil numbers) and place funding (funding for a pre-determined number of places rather than by reference to pupil numbers). In *B v Harrow London Borough* Council (No. 1) [2000] 1 WLR, the House of Lords held it was right to have regard to the fact that a funded special school place would go unfilled were a child to attend an out-of-area school. In *Oxfordshire County Council v GB & Others* [2001] EWCA Civ 1358, Sedley LJ set out his understanding of *Harrow* at [14]: "if unused special school places represent a loss which can be made good by making efficient use of them, then letting the child be unnecessarily placed elsewhere is an inefficient use of such resources". Later Sedley LJ set out his 'additional burden' approach.

As with assessing the 'cost' of educating a child at a maintained mainstream school, the starting point should be the legislative scheme for funding maintained schools: at [42]. Under the School and Early Years Finance (England) Regulations 2013, in the case of a mainstream school with reserved places for children with SEN, neither these places nor children occupying the places attracted an 'AWPU' amount because the 'AWPU' equation subtracted reserved places from pupil numbers: at [57]. A sum for each reserved place was included in the school's budget share whether or not the place was filled: at [58-59]. Maintained special schools also received a budget share and local authorities had to include a sum for each place, and funding was determined by reference to places not to pupil numbers: at [60].

The cost involved in educating a young person in further education

In *PM v Worcestershire County Council* [2022] UKUT 53 (AAC) the young person in question wished to attend an independent learning provider approved under section 41 of 2014 Act; the local authority contended this would be incompatible with the efficient use of resources under section 39(4)(b)(ii) and proposed a college of further education. Mitchell J considered how the costs of each placement should be assessed. Subsections 14(1) and (2) of the Education Act 2002 confer a power on the Secretary of State to give, or make arrangements for the giving of, financial assistance to any person for or in connection with purposes which include the provision of education or educational services (apart from higher education). Section 100(1)(a) of the Apprenticeships, Skills, Children and Learning Act 2009 confers power on the Secretary of State to secure the provision of financial resources to persons providing education or training within the Secretary of State's remit under Part 4 of the Act. The Education and Skills Funding Agency ("ESFA") is an executive agency of the Department for Education and exercises these powers for the Secretary of State in relation to the funding of further education in England. At the material time, the ESFA's *High Needs Funding 2019 to 2020 Operational Guide* was applicable and the ESFA had also issued *Funding Guidance for Young People 2019 to 2020.*

The parties agreed that: (a) the high needs place-funding streams provided for by the ESFA high needs funding guidance, often referred to as 'element 1' and 'element 2' funding, were not contingent on a student taking up a funded place, because institutions subject to ESFA high needs funding guidance had a certain number of 'pre-funded' places; (b) where a young person proposed to take up a place that attracted element 1 and 2 funding, such funding was to be discounted for purpose of the cost comparison, since the resources represented by such funding would be expended whether or not the young person attended the institution; (c), under ESFA's general funding guidance, funding was linked to a particular student taking up a particular place at an educational institution and places were not 'pre-funded'; this meant that the entire amount of ESFA 'general' funding for a particular placement was to be taken into account for the purposes of section 39(4)(b)(ii). Where the parties *disagreed* was over whether the place at the FE college provisionally allocated to the young person in question attracted element 1 and 2 funding under ESFA's high needs funding guide, or not. Mitchell J stated, at [40], that the ESFA high needs funding guide indicated that it was for LAs to determine "the number of funded places" in their area, therefore it should not be unduly difficult for LAs to supply the First-tier Tribunal with evidence that a particular post-16 institution has designated places for high needs students i.e. that it is one of the learning providers within its area that has been allocated places that attract ESFA high needs funding. It was not argued before the Upper Tribunal that ESFA high needs funding did not fall within the 'resources' to be considered for the purposes of section 39(4)(b)(ii).

There is currently a 2023 to 2024 Operational Guide, updated on 17 January 2023, and ESFA funding guidance for young people 2021 to 2023.

Securing an 'appropriate' school or type of school (or other institution) and the operation of section 33 (securing a 'mainstream' education)

By subsection 83(2) of the 2014 Act "mainstream school" means (a) a maintained school that is not a special school, or (b) an Academy school that is not a special school. By section 337(1) of the 1996 Act a school in England is a special school if it is specially organised to make special educational provision for pupils with special educational needs, and it is (a) maintained by a local authority, (b) an Academy school, or (c) a non-maintained special school.

Subsections 33(1) and (2) of the 2014 provide that in a case within subsections 39(5) or 40(2), the local authority must secure that the EHC plan provides for the child or young person to be educated in a maintained nursery school, mainstream school or mainstream post-16 institution, unless that is incompatible with the wishes of the child's parent or the young person (subsection 33(2(a)), or the provision of efficient education for others (subsection 33(2)(b)).

A local authority may rely on the exception in subsection 33(2)(b) in relation to maintained nursery schools, mainstream schools or mainstream post-16 institutions *in its area taken as a whole* only if it shows that there are no reasonable steps that it could take to prevent the incompatibility: subsection 33(3). In relation to a *particular* mainstream school, mainstream school or mainstream post-16 institution, a LA may rely on the exception in subsection (2)(b) only if it shows that there are no reasonable steps that it or the governing body, proprietor or principal could take to prevent the incompatibility.

In *ME v London Borough of Southwark* [2017] UKUT 73 (AAC) Jacobs J set out how sections 38, 39, 40 and 33 apply and the order in which they must be considered. If parents request their child to attend a specific school (or other institution), whether mainstream or not, under section 38, then section 39 applies. If the local authority does *not* have to accede to the parents' request because a condition in subsection 39(4) applies, the LA must identify a school or type of school that is appropriate for the child (subsection 39(5)). The issue must then be considered further under section 33: at [9]. The LA must secure that the child be educated in a mainstream school unless a condition in subsection 33(2) is satisfied. If parents have not requested a specific school (or other institution) under section 38, then subsection 44(2) applies: again, the LA must identify a school or type of school that is appropriate for the child, and the issue must be considered under section 33: at [10] and [13].

Jacobs J held, at [14], that the word 'appropriate' in subsections 39(5) and 40(2) merely provides a link back to section 33 and operates as a shorthand reference to the requirements of section 33, without adding any additional requirement that has to be satisfied (although he added, "the authority would surely want to take account of the child's age, ability, aptitude and needs"). Section 33 does not contain any express provision that the school or post-16 institution is suitable for the child:

R (MH) v SENDIST and LB of Hounslow [2004] EWCA Civ 770 at [69] and *Bury MBC v SU* [2010] UKUT 406 (AAC) at [7] and [21-22]. Indeed, it was noted in *Bury MBC v SU* at [21] that the Special Educational Needs and Disability Act 2001 had amended section 316 of the 1996 Act (the statutory predecessor to section 33) to remove a condition of compatibility "with [the child] receiving the special educational provision which his learning difficulty calls for". In *Harrow Council* v AM [2013] UKUT 0157 (AAC) Mark J stated, at [27]: "In my judgment, the apparent incompatibility between the provision of suitable education and the requirement to name a mainstream school without express regard to the suitability of the school for the child can only be reconciled on the basis that the local education authority is under an absolute obligation to make a school suitable, if there is no suitable school already, whether inside or outside its area, where the child can be found a place, subject only to the qualification in section 316(3)(b). It has to provide for the identified needs. It cannot say that it will educate the child in a mainstream school without providing for them. Nor can it rely on any independent resources issue in this respect. This combines the need to protect the interests of the child with Parliament's intention, in amending 1996 Act in 2001, to promote inclusion." Jacobs J noted, in *ME v London Borough of Southwark* at [17-18], that section 33 also imposes no condition of compatibility with the efficient use of resources.

Lane J further held, at [12], that *R (MH) v SENDIST v London Borough of Hounslow* at [79-80] is authority for the proposition that sections 39 and 33 are separate, meaning that a school rejected under section 39 may still be named under section 33. In R*(MH)* at [79-80] the Upper Tribunal rejected the submission that where, in the course of the section 316 process, the parent has proposed a particular mainstream school or particular mainstream schools, such expressions of preference fall to be treated as if they had been made in the course of the paragraph 3 process. If that were the correct analysis, the effect would be to reintroduce into section 316 the 'suitability' condition which Parliament specifically removed from the original section 316 when it enacted the 2001 Act. The Upper Tribunal also rejected the submission that such an interpretation of sections 316 and 316A enables a parent to 'bypass' the stricter test laid down by paragraph 3(3). The paragraph 3 process is wholly distinct from the section 316 process. Whereas, under paragraph 3, parents have a qualified right to insist on a placement at the particular school of their choice, in the context of the section 316 process there is no such right. In that context, any preferences expressed by a parent for a particular school or for particular schools are no more than nominations of candidates for consideration in accordance with the section 316/316A criteria. In the context of the section 316 process, the Tribunal must consider all candidates for nomination on an equal footing, whether they are proposed by the parent or by the LEA.

If follows that under the 2014 Act, under section 39, parents have a qualified right to insist on a placement at the particular school of their choice, but in the context of the section 33 process, any preferences expressed by a parent for a particular school or for particular schools are no more than nominations of candidates for consideration in accordance with the section 33 criteria, so the Tribunal must consider all candidates for nomination on an equal footing, whether they are proposed by the parent or by the LA, having regard to the general principle in section 9 where it applies.

Subsection 33(6) expressly states that subsection 33(2) does not prevent the child or young person from being educated in an independent school, a non-maintained special school or a special post-16 institution, if the cost is not to be met by a local authority or the Secretary of State.

If, in a 'Section I' appeal, the Tribunal finds that the school (or other institution) proposed by the local authority is not appropriate in that it cannot meet the child or young person's SEN, it may name the school (or other institution) proposed by the parent or young person if it is satisfied that it is suitable, but it may decide to adjourn to enable the LA to identify another school capable of delivering the special educational provision or name a type: see *Richardson v Solihull* [1998] EWCA Civ 3535 at [51].

Specialist 'units'

A mainstream school may have 'base' or 'unit' within it, and some have SEN-reserved places and there may be other types of 'units' whose 'school' status is unclear. There may be confusion as to whether a 'base' or 'unit' is an entity which can be named in an EHC plan. Two authorities provide some guidance: *TB v Essex CC (SEN)* [2013] UKUT 534 (AAC) and *MA v Borough of Kensington and Chelsea* (SEN) [2015] UKUT 186 (AAC).

In *TB v Essex CC* Lane J considered whether the entity named in Part 4 of a Statement – 'GROW Project '(Grow)' – was a school or other institution within the meaning of section 4 of the 1996 Act, and, if it was, was it lawful to name it in conjunction with another entity, a Pupil Referral Unit, at which the child would be formally registered. There was not a lot of evidence before the First-tier Tribunal as to what 'GROW' was. It was based at WH Academy, and the child would attend 'GROW' there, but the child would not be registered at WH Academy; he would be registered with the LA's Children Support Service, a PRU. Lane J observed, at [15], that the First-tier Tribunal's decision was easy to grasp but hard to categorise in legal terms. The Tribunal clearly intended the child to be registered at a PRU which is a school under section 19 of the 1996 and has powers to send pupils 'off site' for instruction and training. However, all the educational provision for the child would be made 'off-site' on the premises of another school (WHA). Lane J considered whether 'GROW' was a school under section 4 of the 1996 Act and concluded, at [33], that it is not justifiable to "encrust the words 'educational institution' in s. 4 with the technicalities relating to the regulation, governance, financing and administration of schools associated with the various categories recognised for those purposes." That is *not* to say that the technicalities of 'school' or other indicia (for example, whether it has its own site, or is referred to as a 'school' rather than a 'project' or a 'base') are irrelevant: they are factors which are helpful in assessing whether an entity is an educational institution. This is not, however, a tick-box exercise. Depending on the circumstances, a greater or smaller number of factors may serve to answer the question: at [34].

In *MA v Borough of Kensington and Chelsea* (SEN) [2015] UKUT 186 (AAC) the local authority named a unit ('the Grove') at particular maintained school ('the Primary') in a child's statement and parents appealed, arguing that 'the Grove' was in reality a separate special school and that the child had to be educated in a mainstream school unless the conditions in section 316 of the 1996 Act (the statutory predecessor of section 33 of the 2014 Act) were met. The First-tier Tribunal held that 'the Grove' was not a separate school. Levenson J held, at [20], that as the 'mainstream' school that parents wanted was a non-maintained school, the real issue was the application of section 9. Parents did not want their child to attend a special school and if 'the Grove' was in reality a separate special school, the Tribunal's decision could not stand. If 'the Grove' was in reality part of 'the Primary' and therefore part of a maintained school, the Tribunal's decision could stand. Levenson J considered *TB v Essex CC*, noting that section 4 of the 1996 Act defines "school" as meaning a list of particular types of educational institution. Whether an entity is an educational institution of one of those types is then a question of fact for the specialist First-tier Tribunal, which must take account of all the relevant evidence and at least consider the matters in paragraph [34] of *TB v Essex CC* as well as any other factors it considers relevant: [28]. There was no basis for saying that the First-tier Tribunal's conclusion about the nature of 'the Grove' was wrong in law: at [29].

Views of the child or young person

The local authority and the First-tier Tribunal, 'standing in the shoes' of the LA, has an obligation to take the views of the child or young person into account when deciding an appeal. The views of the child or young person will not usually be determinative, although in a particular case, they could be. The First-tier Tribunal's consideration of the views of the child or young person in deciding the appeal is addressed further in Chapter 10.

However, in *St Helen's BC v TE and another* [2018] UKUT 278 (AAC) the First-tier Tribunal concluded that a school was not suitable, having found as fact that the child had formed an entrenched and currently intractable opposition to attending that school or any mainstream provision. The Tribunal made clear in the reasons for its decision that there was no evidence to suggest that the child was being manipulated by his parents or that his opposition to the placement was attributable to opposition on their part. It explained that it was not allowing the child to 'exercise a veto', but that his opposition stemmed from the SEN outlined in his EHC plan, drawing on the undisputed evidence of an educational psychologist. The Upper Tribunal (Ward J) held, at [23], that these were conclusions that were open to a specialist Tribunal on the evidence before it.

Naming a 'type' of school in Section I

By subsection 39(5)(b) of the 2014 Act (or subsection 40(2)(b), where no request for a particular school or other institution was made under section 38) Section I does not have to name a school or other institution: it can specify the type of school or other institution which the local authority thinks would be appropriate for the child or young person. The LA can simply name a type of school or institution and so can the First-tier Tribunal: *R (MH) v SENDIST and LB of Hounslow* [2004] EWCA 770 at [30-32].

The provisions of the 2014 Act and the 1996 Act contain various definitions of different types of school and institution. For example, section 5 of the 1996 Act defines "primary school" and "secondary school". However, there is nothing in the legislation which expressly provides that, for the purposes of subsections 35(5)(b) or subsection 40(2)(b) of the 2014 Act, the 'type' of school or other institution must be specified with reference to any of these definitions. Also, there is little guidance in the case law. In *R (M) v East Sussex* [2009] EWHC 1651 at [12] the High Court indicated that 'maintained special primary school' is a 'type' distinct from 'a maintained special secondary school'. That was a case in which the child's statement named a school but failed to specify the type of school it was. As the named school made provision for child ages 5-16, when the child reached the age of secondary transfer, and the local authority made no amendments to the statement, this prevented the parents from launching an appeal against the contents of the statement in order to request a different school for the secondary phase (the position would have been different under the 2014 Act Part 3, as section 51(2)(e) affords a right of appeal after a review of an EHC plan where no amendments are made).

Where an EHC plan does not name a school or institution and only specifies a type, there is obvious potential for problems. The local authority must still secure the specified special educational provision for the child or young person at a school or other institution of that type (section 42 of the 2014 Act) and there will be no school or other institution with a duty to admit the child under section 43. In R *(MH) v SENDIST and LB of Hounslow* [2004] EWCA 770 at [76-78] the Court of Appeal held that although there was no *duty* in law to name a particular school, the statutory guidance which then applied was to the effect that a local authority should nevertheless normally exercise its *power* to do so. It added, at [77]: "The conclusion that the power to name a particular school should normally be exercised is in our judgment reinforced by a consideration of the practicalities of the situation. At some stage, a placement must be made in a particular school. It is, as it seems to us, plainly desirable that that placement should be specified... not least because... the parent will then have a right of appeal against it..."

Where parents have opposing views on placement

The 2014 Act does not explicitly provide for the situation where parents disagree on which of two suitable schools should be named in their child's EHC plan, nor does the SEND Code of Practice 2015 provide any relevant guidance. Fortunately, in *S-G v (1) Denbighshire County Council* (2*) (B)* (SEN) [2016] UKUT 0460 (AAC) Mitchell J gave some general guidance to Tribunals about dealing with such cases. That case concerned an appeal to the Special Educational Needs Tribunal for Wales under the Education Act 1996. The father appealed in relation to the school named in the child's statement, 'P School', asking for a different school to be named. The mother provided a statement for the proceedings; her view was that 'P School' should be named, but she chose not to be a party to the appeal. There was a joint residence order in place in respect of the child.

Mitchell J noted, at [40-43], that the family court had the power to make a 'prohibited steps' order or a 'specific issue' order as defined by section 8 of the Children Act 1989 on application, or in ongoing family proceedings (section 10(1) of the 1989 Act). SENTW had no statutory power to *transfer* SEN proceedings to the family court with a view to the family court making a section 8 order to resolve a parental education dispute. It might be appropriate for SENTW to *adjourn* an appeal pending resolution of family proceedings concerned with the exercise of parental responsibility in relation to a child's education. However, if a Tribunal were considering such a step, it should take into account (a) that the family court did not have power to direct a local authority to make changes to a statement or to require a Tribunal to exercise its functions in any particular way; (b) where parents disagreed over two suitable maintained schools (both of which are the subject of what would normally be an operative parental preference), the family court might think a specialist tribunal was better placed to determine which school is best for the child; (c) not infrequently, fathers do not have parental responsibility for their children and, if a father did not have parental responsibility, a section 8 order might not assist a Tribunal in its task of deciding which school to specify in Part 4 of a statement of SEN. However, fathers do have rights as 'parents' under the education legislation whether or not they have parental responsibility.

Mitchell J also pointed out that the Tribunal could decide simply to specify a *type* of school and it would not be within its remit to deal with any subsequent dispute as to the actual school to be attended. Mitchell J further held, at [82-83], that Parliament cannot have intended for the Schedule 27 requirement to specify a parent's preferred maintained school to operate in cases involving a parental dispute over which suitable maintained school to name. Consequently, since Schedule 27 did not require a school to be named in this child's statement, once the SENTW had decided to name a school (rather than a type of school), section 324(4)(b) of the 1996 Act required it to specify the school it considered "appropriate". Mitchell J went on to state, at [84-87], that there is no single model of maintained school; different schools will have different strengths and weaknesses. Even if two maintained schools are both capable of providing a suitable education for a child, it is open to a parent, in cases such as this, to argue that one school would provide a better education than the other: the statutory scheme does not prevent such an argument. Mitchell J held, at [90], that "any educationally relevant matter may be taken into account in deciding which school is appropriate to specify. That could include transport matters and a child's practical living arrangements."

It may be argued that *SG v Denbighshire* should be applied in 'Section I' appeals under the 2014 Act where parents do not agree on placement, so that the requirement in section 39(3) to secure that the EHC plan names the school or other institution specified in the appellant's request does not operate, and the First-tier Tribunal must decide which school is most appropriate.

Mitchell J did not expressly consider the operation of section 9 of the Education Act 1996.

Powers of the First-tier Tribunal in 'Section I' appeals, and compliance

By regulation 43(1) of the 2014 Regulations, before determining any appeal, the First-tier Tribunal may, with the agreement of the parties, correct any deficiencies in the EHC Plan which relate to the SEN or special educational provision for the child or the young person.

By regulation 43(2)(a) and (g), when determining a 'Section I' appeal under section 51(2)(c)(iii) or (iv) or (e) of the 2014 Act, the powers of First-tier Tribunal include the power to dismiss the appeal, or to order the local authority to substitute in the EHC Plan the school or other institution or the type of school or other institution specified in the EHC plan. Where appropriate, this may include naming a special school or institution approved under section 41 where a mainstream school or mainstream post-16 institution is specified in the EHC Plan; or a mainstream school or mainstream post-16 institution where a special school or institution approved under section 41 is specified in the EHC Plan: regulation 43(2)(h).

By regulation 44(2)(f), where the order requires the local authority to amend the name of the school or other institution or the type of school or other institution specified in the EHC plan, the LA shall issue the amended EHC plan within 2 weeks of the order being made. Regulation 44(2) is subject to any direction made by the First-tier Tribunal: regulation 44(1).

In an unopposed appeal, by regulation 45, the Tribunal is not required to make an order. By regulation 45(4), if the appeal is made under section 51(2)(e) of the 2014 Act, the local authority must issue the amended EHC plan to those specified in regulation 22(3) within 5 weeks of the date it notifies the First-tier Tribunal that it will not oppose the appeal before it submits a response. By regulation 45(5), if the appeal is made under section 51(2)(c)(iii) or (iv), the LA must issue the amended EHC plan to those specified in regulation 22(3) within 2 weeks of the date it notifies the First-tier Tribunal that it will not oppose the appeal; or, where the LA is also required to amend the EHC plan in a 'Section B' or 'F' appeal under section 51(2)(c)(i) or (ii), within 5 weeks of the date it notifies the First-tier Tribunal that it will not oppose the appeal.

CHAPTER SEVEN

EDUCATION OTHERWISE THAN AT SCHOOL ('EOTAS')

This chapter addresses the special situation provided for by section 61 of the Children and Families Act 2014 whereby special educational provision may be made for a child or young person 'otherwise' than in a school or post-16 institution or a place at which relevant early years education is provided. This type of provision is sometimes referred to by the shorthand 'EOTAS'. Appeals under section 51 where the parent or young person seeks 'EOTAS' will affect what is specified (or not specified) in Sections F and I of the EHC plan.

Subsection 61(1) of the 2014 Act ("Special educational provision otherwise than in schools, post-16 institutions etc") provides that a local authority in England may arrange for any special educational provision that it has decided is necessary for a child or young person for whom it is responsible to be made "otherwise than in a school or post-16 institution or a place at which relevant early years education is provided." However, a LA may do so "only if satisfied that it would be inappropriate for the provision to be made in a school or post-16 institution or at such a place": subsection 61(2). Before doing so, the authority must consult the child's parent or the young person: subsection 61(3).

By section 4 of the 1996 Act, a 'school' is defined as an educational institution which is outside the further education sector and the higher education sector and is an 'institution' for providing (a) primary education; (b) secondary education; or (c) both primary and secondary education. In *MA v Borough of Kensington and Chelsea (SEN)* [2015] UKUT 0186 (AAC) Levenson J stated at [28] that whether an entity is a school as defined by section 4 is a question of fact for the specialist tribunal, taking account of all the relevant evidence including, where relevant, those factors set out by Lane J at [33] of *TB v Essex County Council (SEN)* [2013] UKUT 0534 (AAC), namely: regulation, governance, financing and administration.

In *Derbyshire County Council v EM and DM (SEN)* [2019] UKUT 240 Wright J stated at [18] that 'a school' in section 61(2) is in effect to be read as 'any school': "It cannot be the case that section 61(2) of the CFA is satisfied, and special educational provision is made otherwise than in school simply if it would be inappropriate for the necessary special educational provision to be made in one school alone but where provision could be appropriately made in another school. Such a reading of the CFA would allow sections 39(5) or 40(2) of that Act to apply at the same time as section 61, which would be an irrational reading of the Act." In *NN -v- Cheshire East Council (SEN)* [2021] UKUT 220 (AAC) at [28], 'in passing', Rowley J agreed.

The term 'inappropriate' was considered by the Court of Appeal in *TM v London Borough of Hounslow* [2009] EWCA Civ 859 which considered section 319 of the 1996 Act (the statutory 'predecessor' to section 61). In *NN v Cheshire East Council (SEN)* [2021] UKUT 220 (AAC) Rowley J considered at [30-31] whether *TM v London Borough of Hounslow* was a relevant authority for the interpretation of section 61 given that the wording of the two sections is not identical, and concluded that it was.

In *TM v London Borough of Hounslow* the Court of Appeal stated, at [26]:

> "The question that the LEA has to address is, therefore, is it satisfied that it would be 'inappropriate' for the special educational provisions of the particular child to be made in a school or not? In answering that question… it is not enough for the LEA to ask simply 'can' the school meet the statement of needs set out in Part 3 of the s 324 statement… if a LEA is to give full effect to the word 'inappropriate', it has to see if a school would 'not be suitable' or 'would not be proper'. To do that… the LEA has to take into account all the circumstances of the case in hand. These circumstances might include, without giving any exhaustive list,

> (which must depend on the facts of the case) consideration of the following matters: the child's background and medical history; the particular educational needs of the child; the facilities that can be provided by a school; the facilities that could be provided other than in a school; the comparative cost of the possible alternatives to the child's educational provisions; the child's reaction to education provisions, either at a school or elsewhere; the parents' wishes; and any other particular circumstances that apply to a particular child."

This exercise must include a consideration of the parents' wishes under section 9 of the 1996 Act, although parental wishes cannot be determinative, except in the very rare case where there are otherwise equally balanced alternatives for the child's special educational needs: *NN v Cheshire East Council (SEN)* [2021] UKUT 220 (AAC) at [27].

In *NN v Cheshire East Council (SEN)* [2021] UKUT 220 (AAC) at [40], Rowley J agreed with the judgment of Wright J in *Derbyshire County Council v EM and DM (SEN)* [2019] UKUT 240 that the earlier Upper Tribunal decision of *M & M v West Sussex County Council (SEN)* [2018] UKUT 347 (AAC) was not correctly decided, and that there is no absolute requirement that all EHC plans must name a school or other institution (or a type of either). Wright J reasoned that if a local authority thinks that no school or other institution (or type of either) would be appropriate for the child or young person, the 'naming' duty under sections 39(5) and 40(2), and thus in Section I of an EHC plan, cannot as a matter of law arise. In a case where, although it is hoped that the child will at some point in the future be able to attend school, it is impossible to predict what type of school would eventually be appropriate for the child, it would be at the very least pointless to name a school or a type of school in Section I of the child's EHC plan in circumstances where no one knows whether that school or type of school will ever be appropriate for him or her; in a case where everyone is agreed that the child will never be able to attend school it would be absurd to name a school or type of school. Parliament cannot have intended such pointless or absurd outcomes.

Regulation 12(1)(i) of the 2014 Regulations requires the EHC plan to set out, in Section I, the name or type of school 'to be attended by' the child. In *East Sussex County Council v TW* [2016] UKUT 528 Jacobs J held, at [32], that it is not a proper use of language to say that a young person's home is somewhere 'to be attended by' him, and that a Tribunal may not add additional information about provision to Section I. In *NN v Cheshire East Council* at [43] Rowley J concluded that there is nothing in the context of regulation 12 which indicates that 'to be attended by' means anything other than its clear and unambiguous meaning of 'to be present at'. Section I must be limited to what is provided by regulation 12(1)(i), i.e. the name of the school and type of school to be attended by the child, or where the name of the school is not specified, the type of school to be attended by the child. Anything which is added to that, for whatever reason, is likely to be classified as an error of law: *NN v Cheshire East Council* at [46].

Against this background, Rowley J, at [47], gave guidance to tribunals considering cases where bespoke provision of education outside a conventional classroom setting and education otherwise than at school are proposed by the parties.

Firstly, the Tribunal must consider section 61 CFA 2014. It must separately ask whether it is satisfied that it would be inappropriate for (i) *any* special educational provision that it has decided is necessary for the child to be made in any school and (ii) any *part* of the provision to be made in any school.

Secondly, in considering these questions, the Tribunal must ask if a school would 'not be suitable' or would 'not be proper'. To do that, it has to take into account all the circumstances of the case. Without being an exhaustive list, those circumstances might include: the child's background and medical history; the particular educational needs of the child; the facilities that can be provided by a school; the facilities that could be provided other than in a school; the comparative cost of the possible alternatives to the child's educational provisions, either at school or elsewhere; the parents' wishes (although they are not generally determinative); and any other particular circumstances that apply to a particular child (*TM v London Borough of Hounslow*).

If the Tribunal is satisfied that it would be inappropriate for *any* such special educational provision to be made in any school, then Section I must be left blank.

Conversely, if the Tribunal is not satisfied that it would be inappropriate for any such special educational provision to be made in any school, it follows that a particular school or type of school would be appropriate for the child (*Derbyshire County Council v EM and DM (SEN)*) in relation to at least part of the provision to be made. This will lead to consideration of what should be specified in Section I of the EHC plan. That, in turn, will involve consideration of regulation 12 of the 2014 Regulations.

If a particular educational institution is proposed, and if it is in issue as to whether or not that institution is a 'school', the Tribunal must consider whether it falls within the definition of a 'school' as set out section 4 of the 1996 Act. This is a question of fact to be determined in the light of all the evidence including, where relevant, matters such as regulation governance, financing and administration (see *MA v Borough of Kensington and Chelsea (SEN)* [2015] UKUT 186 (AAC) and *TB v Essex County Council (SEN)* [2013] UKUT 534 (AAC)).

If it is in issue, the Tribunal must consider whether the school or type of school will be 'attended by' the child. If it is satisfied that the child will be present at a school or type of school for at least part of the time, that is sufficient and so the school or type of school must be specified in Section I. Attending provision provided by the school as part of a bespoke package outside a conventional classroom setting will nonetheless mean that the school is to be attended by the child within the meaning of regulation 12(1)(i).

What is specified in Section I must be strictly limited to the name of the school and type of school to be attended by the child, or where the name of the school is not specified, the type of school to be attended by the child. No more and no less.

For the avoidance of doubt, education in a child's home cannot be named in Section I (*East Sussex County Council v TW* (see above)).

Any special educational provision which will be made otherwise than in a school or type of school will be set out in Section F.

In *DM v Cornwall CC* (SEN) [2022] UKUT 230 (AAC) the Upper Tribunal was tasked with addressing 'specificity' in an EHC plan in the context of 'education otherwise than in school'. The appellant contended that the need for specificity would be greater in that context than where a child was being educated in a school. The Upper Tribunal, at [7], acknowledged that, in a very general sense, educational provision which is bounded by a school building and the provision and rules that may apply to all pupils in that school may to an extent be assumed, and will not need to be stated, whereas that provision *may* need to appear more explicitly in a case where the EHC plan concerns a child being educated at home and otherwise than in school. However, the degree of specificity that is required for an individual child in their EHC plan will always have to depend on the facts of that child's case.

Paragraph 10.31 of the SEND Code of Practice 2015 states that in cases where local authorities and parents agree that home education is the right provision for a child or young person with an EHC plan, the plan should make clear that the child or young person will be educated at home. If it does, then, under section 42(2), the LA must arrange the special educational provision set out in the plan, working with the parents. The Code contrasts this situation with cases where the EHC plan gives the name of a school or type of school where the child will be educated but parents decide to educate at home. In this situation, the LA is not under a duty to make the special educational provision set out in the plan *provided* it is satisfied that the arrangements made by the parents are suitable, and it must still review the plan annually to assure itself that the provision set out in it continues to be appropriate and that the child's SEN continue to be met: paragraph 10.32. Where the LA has decided that the provision is appropriate, it should amend the plan to name the type of school that would be suitable but state that parents have made their own arrangements under section 7 of the Education Act 1996:

paragraph 10.32. Paragraphs 10.30 to 10.38 give further guidance in relation to the situation where parents 'electively' home educate.

The SEND Code of Practice, at paragraphs 10.39 to 10.52, also addresses the situation of children with SEN who are in 'alternative provision', including those who are in 'alternative provision' because of health needs.

Section 19(1) of the Education Act 1996 ('Exceptional provision of education in pupil referral units or elsewhere: England') requires local authorities to make arrangements for the provision of suitable education at school or otherwise than at school for those children of compulsory school age who, "by reason of illness, exclusion from school or otherwise, may not for any period receive suitable education unless such arrangements are made for them." The education to be provided for a child in pursuance of arrangements made by a LA under subsection 19(1) must be "full-time education" unless the LA considers that, for reasons which relate to the physical or mental health of the child, it would not be in the child's best interests for full-time education to be provided for the child. In that situation, the education may be on such part-time basis as the LA considers to be in the child's best interests: subsections 19(3A) and (3AA). "Suitable education" in this context means "efficient education suitable to [the child's] age, ability and aptitude and to any special educational needs [the child] may have". Currently, there is no statutory definition of "full-time" education. The section 19(1) duty does not apply in the case of a child who will cease to be of compulsory school age within the next six weeks and does not have any public examinations or other assessments for which the child has been entered to complete: section 19(2).

By subsection 19(4) of the 1996 Act, a local authority in England *may* make arrangements for the provision of suitable education otherwise than at school for those *young persons* who, by reason of illness, exclusion from school or otherwise, may not for any period receive suitable education unless such arrangements are made for them.

By subsection 19(2B) of the 1996 Act, any school established in England and maintained by a local authority in England which is specially organised to provide education for such children, and is not a community or foundation school, a community or foundation special school, or a maintained nursery school, shall be known as a "pupil referral unit". A LA in England may secure the provision of boarding accommodation at any pupil referral unit. Further provisions relating to PRUs are found in Schedule 1 of the 1996 Act.

By subsection 19(5) of the 1996 Act, any child for whom education is provided otherwise than at school in pursuance of section 19, and any young person for whom full-time education is so provided in pursuance of this section, shall be treated for the purposes of the 1996 Act as a pupil. This means that the provisions of section 9 of the 1996 Act (the duty to have regard to the general principle that pupils are to be educated in accordance with the wishes of their parents, so far as that is compatible with the provision of efficient instruction and training and the avoidance of unreasonable public expenditure) will apply in such cases.

The Department for Education has published statutory guidance for local authorities, "Ensuring a good education for children who cannot attend school because of health needs".

Orders of the First-tier Tribunal and compliance in an 'EOTAS' case

Because any special educational provision which will be made otherwise than in a school or type of school will be set out in Section F, it follows that the orders of the First-tier Tribunal and compliance will be as per a 'Section F' appeal: see further, Chapter 5. If the outcome of the appeal is that the Tribunal names a school or type of school (or other institution) in Section I, it follows that the orders of the First-tier Tribunal and compliance will be as per a 'Section I' appeal.

CHAPTER EIGHT

CEASING TO MAINTAIN EHC PLANS AND 'CEASING TO MAINTAIN' APPEALS

Sections 45 and 46 of the Children and Families Act 2014 Part 3 and regulations 29, 30, 31 of the Special Educational Needs and Disability Regulations 2014 are the key provisions which govern decisions to cease to maintain EHC plans. The key provisions of the SEND Code of Practice are at paragraphs 9.199 to 9.210. In addition, the Department of Education has published relevant non-statutory guidance, "SEND: 19- to 25-year-olds' entitlement to EHC plans" published 21 February 2017.

Subsections 51(1) and 51(2)(f) of the 2014 Act makes provision for a child's parent or a young person to appeal to the First-tier Tribunal against a decision of a local authority under section 45 to cease to maintain an EHC plan for the child or young person (subject to mediation). Often an appeal against a decision to cease to maintain an EHC plan will be brought alongside a 'Section B', 'F' or 'I' appeal against the contents of the existing plan.

Subsections 45(1), (2) and (3) of the 2014 Act provide:

> (1) A local authority may cease to maintain an EHC plan for a child or young person only if—
>
> > (a) the authority is no longer responsible for the child or young person, or
> >
> > (b) the authority determines that it is no longer necessary for the plan to be maintained.

(2) The circumstances in which it is no longer necessary for an EHC plan to be maintained for a child or young person include where the child or young person no longer requires the special educational provision specified in the plan.

(3) When determining whether a young person aged over 18 no longer requires the special educational provision specified in his or her EHC plan, a local authority must have regard to whether the educational or training outcomes specified in the plan have been achieved.

By section 45(4), a local authority may *not* cease to maintain an EHC plan for a child or young person *until* (a) after the end of the period allowed for bringing an appeal under section 51 against its decision to cease to maintain the plan, where no such appeal is brought before the end of that period; (b) after the appeal has been finally determined, where such an appeal is brought before the end of that period.

Regulations 29 and 30 of the 2014 Regulations make different provision for children or young people under the age of 18, and for young people aged 18 or over.

By regulation 29, a local authority may not cease to maintain an EHC plan for a child or young person under the age of 18 unless it determines that it is "no longer necessary for special educational provision to be made for the child or young person in accordance with an EHC plan". By regulation 29(2), where a child or young person under the age of 18 is not receiving education or training, the LA must review the EHC plan in accordance with regulations 18 and 19 and amend it in accordance with regulation 22 where appropriate, to ensure that the young person continues to receive education or training.

By regulation 30(1) of the 2014 Regulations, when a young person aged 18 or over ceases to attend the educational institution specified in his or her EHC plan, so is no longer receiving education or training, a local authority may not cease to maintain that EHC plan, unless it has reviewed that EHC plan in accordance with regulations 18 and 19 and ascertained that the young person does not wish to return to education or training, either at the educational institution specified in the EHC plan, or otherwise, or determined that returning to education or training would not be appropriate for the young person. In *B & M v Cheshire East Council* [2018] UKUT 232 (AAC) at [98-99] Mitchell J commented that regulation 30(1) is somewhat puzzling, as it presupposes that the education or training of a young person with an EHC plan has stopped, yet the whole purpose of an EHC plan is to ensure that a young person receives education or training and, if the statutory process has been followed, one would normally expect the plan to cease upon a young person's planned departure from an educational institution without transferring to another institution. It might be thought that regulation 30(1) is intended to deal with sudden departures from education, not anticipated by the statutory process.

By regulation 30(2), where, following the review, the local authority ascertains that the young person wishes to return to education or training either at the educational institution specified in the EHC plan, or at another educational institution, and determines that it is appropriate for the young person to do so, it must amend the young person's EHC plan as it thinks necessary in accordance with regulation 22.

Regulation 31 makes provision for the procedure for determining whether to cease to maintain an EHC plan.

The SEND Code of Practice confirms, at paragraph 9.200, that local authorities must *not* cease to maintain an EHC plan simply because the young person is aged 19 or over. The Code also confirms, at paragraph 9.204, that a LA will not be able to cease an EHC plan because a child or young person is in custody. The Code states, at paragraph 9.207, that support should generally cease at the end of the academic year, to allow young people to complete their programme of study. Paragraph 9.207 further states that it is important that a child or young person's exit from an EHC plan is planned carefully, to support smooth transitions and effective preparation for adulthood. Where a young person aged 18 or over is in receipt of adult services, the local authority should ensure that adult services are involved in and made aware of the decision to cease to maintain the plan: paragraph 9.208. Moreover, where the care part of an EHC plan is provided by adult services under the Care Act 2014 because the person is 18 or over, the care plan will remain in place when the other elements of the EHC plan cease, and there will be no requirement for the young person to be re-assessed at this point, unless there is reason to re-assess him or her for health and social care because their circumstances have changed: paragraph 9.210. See also sections 17ZG, 17ZH and 17ZI of the Children Act 1989.

In *B & M v Cheshire East Council* [2018] UKUT 232 (AAC) a local authority decided to cease to maintain the EHC plan of a severely disabled young person aged 19, Ms M, after she ceased her sixth form at a special school. The adult social care department of the LA prepared a care and support plan for her under the Care Act 2014. It was submitted on behalf of Ms M that the LA should continue to maintain the EHC plan and that she should attend a specialist college. However, the LA argued that Ms M had met the outcomes specified in her EHC plan, that she no longer needed to be in 'formal education', and that adult social care day services, which would provide 'suitable activities and learning opportunities', were suitable to meet her needs.

Mitchell J, at [83-85], addressed the relevance of a young person's achievement of EHC plan outcomes when a local authority is considering whether to continue to maintain a plan. Section 45(3) requires the LA to "have regard" to whether the educational or training outcomes in the EHC plan have been achieved, so in this respect the 2014 Act influences the LA's thought processes rather than mandating a particular result. It does not follow that where outcomes have been achieved, it is no longer necessary to maintain the plan. The *achievement* of outcomes *may* indicate that a young person no longer requires the special educational provision specified in the EHC plan and that it is no longer necessary to maintain the plan. However, this will depend on a range of considerations, including for example the young person's educational and training aspirations, the reasons why outcomes were achieved and whether the young person's special educational needs profile has altered. *Failure* to achieve outcomes does not inevitably render it necessary to *maintain* a young person's EHC plan. For one thing, the young person may not wish to remain in education or training, but even if they do, the reasons why one or more outcome was not achieved, the type of education or training proposed, and the young person's current SEN profile are all examples of facts that may, in a particular case, tend to show that, despite outcomes not being achieved, it is no longer necessary to maintain an EHC plan.

Mitchell J also considered, at [91-92], that there is an 'affinity' between the test for deciding whether to cease to maintain an EHC plan and the test under section 37(1) for deciding whether to prepare and maintain an EHC plan in the first place, whether it is 'necessary' for special educational provision to be made in accordance with an EHC plan. In deciding whether to cease to maintain an EHC plan, a local authority should ask itself whether the person would meet the test for preparing and maintaining an EHC plan in the first instance. LAs should consider whether they have sufficient up-to-date information about a young person before deciding to cease to maintain an EHC plan. Mitchell J also held, at [93], that Ms M's Care Act 2014 assessment was not, and could not have been, an assessment of her educational needs.

The non-statutory guidance, "SEND: 19- to 25-year-olds' entitlement to EHC plans" states (in section 1), "The majority of young people with EHC plans complete further education with their peers by age 19, and our expectation is that this will continue. However, we recognise that some young people with SEND need longer to complete and consolidate their education and training. The length of time will vary according to each young person, and judgements on when to stop or maintain a plan must be made on a case-by-case basis and in accordance with the statutory tests and processes (see section 45 of the Children and Families Act 2014 and paragraphs 9.199 – 9.210 of the SEND Code of Practice)."

When the authority is "no longer responsible" for the child or young person

As set out in Chapter 1, section 24 of the 2014 Act states that a local authority is "responsible" for a child or young person if he or she "is in the authority's area and has been (a) identified by the authority as someone who has or may have special educational needs, or (b) brought to the authority's attention by any person as someone who has or may have special educational needs."

Accordingly, the circumstances where a local authority is no longer responsible for a child or young person include where the child or young person has moved to another LA area. However, regulation 15 of the 2014 Regulations provides for the transfer of EHC plans from one local authority to another where a child or young person in respect of whom an EHC plan is maintained moves from the area of the LA which maintains the EHC plan into the area of another LA. Chapter 1 addresses the law in relation to whether a child or young person is or is not "in the area" of a particular LA, and the operation of regulation 15.

The circumstances where a local authority is no longer responsible for a young person also include where the young person enters higher education (see the Code of Practice, paragraph 9.201). Higher education is excluded from the definition of special educational needs by section 83(4) of the 2014 Act.

Paragraph 9.201 of the SEND Code of Practice states that the circumstances where a local authority is no longer responsible for a young person also include where a young person aged 16 or over leaves education to take up paid employment (including employment with training but excluding apprenticeships) and where the young person is aged 18 or over and leaves education and no longer wishes to engage in further learning. However, in accordance with regulation 30, the LA must not cease to maintain the plan unless it has first reviewed the plan to determine whether the young person wishes to return to education or training, either at the educational institution specified in the plan or somewhere else, and if the young person does wish to return to education or training, and the LA thinks it appropriate for the young person to do so, it must amend the young person's EHC plan as it thinks necessary, and it must maintain the plan. The Code adds that the LA should seek to re-engage the young person in education or training as soon as possible: paragraph 9.203.

Maintaining, or ceasing to maintain, an EHC plan after a young person's 25th birthday

Section 83(2) states that "young person" means a person over compulsory school age but *under 25*. However, by section 46 of the 2014 Act ('Maintaining an EHC plan after young person's 25th birthday'), a local authority may continue to maintain an EHC plan for a young person until the end of the academic year during which the young person attains the age of 25.

By section 46(2), "Academic year" means the period of twelve months ending on the prescribed date, and by regulation 46 of the 2014 Regulations, an academic year for the purpose of section 46 is the period of twelve months which ends: (a) in relation to a young person attending an institution within the further education sector, on 31st July; (b) in relation to a young person receiving apprenticeship training (having the same meaning as in section 83(5) of the Apprenticeships, Skills, Children and Learning Act 2009) on the date that that apprenticeship training finishes, or on the day before the young person attains the age of 26 if earlier; (c) in all other cases, on the day that the young person's course of education or training is scheduled to end, or on the day before the young person attains the age of 26 if earlier.

In *JL (by EA) v Somerset County Council* [2021] UKUT 324 (AAC) at [23] Ward J declined to decide whether, when a local authority wishes to terminate a plan following a person's 25th birthday, it is obliged to go through the "ceasing to maintain" provisions of section 45, but stated, at [28]: "Whether ceasing to maintain a plan by virtue of a decision not to exercise the s.46 power is subject to the s.45 procedure will have to await another case but if it is not, the decision will be subject to the normal constraints of administrative law and justiciable, though not by the FtT, by the Administrative Court or by this Chamber on a discretionary transfer to it under s.31A(3) of the Senior Courts Act 1981."

In *JL (by EA) v Somerset CC* it was submitted to the First-tier Tribunal on behalf of the young person, J, that his EHC plan should be extended beyond the date when he would cease to be a "young person" by virtue of section 83(2) of the 2014 Act, because a supported internship, which had been a key part of his special educational provision, had not materialised in the form anticipated (instead being restricted to remote working and with reduced hours) as a consequence of the Covid-19 pandemic. The First-tier Tribunal did not think that it could specify this provision because it had no jurisdiction to order the local authority to extend the EHC Plan. Ward J, at [25-28], agreed that the First-tier Tribunal has no jurisdiction to order the local authority to extend the plan, but this does not mean that the Tribunal cannot specify a course or an internship which, if adequately completed, would end on a date after the young person in question would cease to be a "young person". The possibility of extension of the end date via section 46 and regulation 46 will be a relevant factor for the First-tier Tribunal to take into account in cases where it arises.

Powers of the First-tier Tribunal in 'ceasing to maintain' appeals, and compliance

By regulation 43(1) of the 2014 Regulations, before determining any appeal, the First-tier Tribunal may, with the agreement of the parties, correct any deficiencies in the EHC Plan which relate to the SEN or special educational provision for the child or the young person.

By regulation 43(2)(a), when determining an appeal under subsection 51(2)(f) the powers of the First-tier Tribunal include the power to dismiss the appeal (reg. 42(2(a)); or to order the local authority to continue to maintain the EHC Plan in its existing form where the LA has refused to do (reg. 42(2)(e)); or to order the LA to continue to maintain the EHC Plan with amendments so far as that relates to either the assessment of SEN or the special educational provision, and make any other consequential amendments as the Tribunal thinks fit (reg. 43(2)(f)); or to order the LA to substitute in the EHC Plan the school or other institution or the type of school or other institution specified in the EHC plan (reg. 43(2)(g)). Where appropriate, this may include naming a special school or institution approved under section 41 where a mainstream school or mainstream post-16 institution is specified in the EHC Plan; or a mainstream school or mainstream post-16 institution where a special school or institution approved under section 41 is specified in the EHC Plan (reg. 43(2)(g)).

By regulation 44(2)(a), where the order dismisses an appeal against a determination to cease an EHC Plan, the local authority shall cease to maintain the EHC Plan immediately. By regulation 44(2)(g), where the order requires the LA to continue to maintain the EHC Plan in its existing form, the LA shall continue to maintain the EHC Plan. Where the order requires the LA to continue and amend the EHC Plan, the LA shall continue to maintain the EHC Plan and amend the EHC Plan within 5 weeks of the order being made: regulation 44(2)(h).

In an unopposed appeal, by regulation 45, the Tribunal is not required to make an order. By regulation 45(6A) in a 'ceasing to maintain' appeal made under section 51(2)(f) of the 2014 Act, the local authority must continue to maintain the EHC plan, and where the LA has also agreed to amend the EHC plan, the LA must amend it within 5 weeks of the date it notifies the First-tier Tribunal that it will not oppose the appeal before it submits a response.

CHAPTER NINE

HEALTH AND SOCIAL CARE NEEDS AND PROVISION AND 'EXTENDED APPEALS'

This chapter addresses the ways in which questions relating to health and social care needs and provision may arise in appeals to the First-tier Tribunal under section 51 of the Children and Families Act 2014. It also addresses appeals to the First-tier Tribunal under section 51 which include health or social care aspects, known as 'extended appeals,' and the powers conferred on the First-Tier Tribunal by the Special Educational Needs and Disability (First-tier Tribunal Recommendations Power) Regulations 2017.

Key legislation includes Part 3 of the 2014 Act, the Special Educational Needs and Disability Regulations 2014, the National Health Service Act 2006, the Children Act 1989, the Chronically Sick and Disabled Person Act 1970, the Care Act 2014 and the Special Educational Needs and Disability (First-tier Tribunal Recommendations Power) Regulations 2017. In addition, the Department for Education has issued guidance, "SEND Tribunal: extended appeals – Guidance for local authorities, health commissioners, parents and young people" dated September 2021 ("the Guidance").

An EHC needs assessment, by section 36 of the 2014 Act, includes an assessment of the health care and social care needs of a child or young person.

An EHC plan, by subsections 37(2)(d), (e) and (f) of the 2014 Act, specifies any health care provision reasonably required by the learning difficulties and disabilities which result in the child or young person having SEN; in the case of a child or a young person aged under 18, any social care provision which must be made for him or her by the local authority as a result of section 2 of the Chronically Sick and Disabled Persons Act 1970; and any social care provision reasonably required by the learning difficulties and disabilities which result in the child or young person having SEN, to the extent that the provision is not already specified in the plan under 37(2)(e). By regulations 12(c), (d), (g) and (h) of the 2014 Regulations, the EHC plan must set out the child or young person's health care needs which relate to their SEN (in Section C of the plan), any health care provision reasonably required by the learning difficulties and disabilities which result in him or her having SEN (in Section G), the child or young person's social care needs which relate to their special educational needs or disability (in Section D), in the case of a child or young person aged under 18, any social care provision which must be made for him or her by the LA as a result of section 2 of the Chronically Sick and Disabled Persons Act 1970 (in Section H1), and any other social care provision reasonably required by the learning difficulties and disabilities which result in the child or young person having SEN (in Section H2).

Section 21 of the 2014 Act defines "health care provision" and "social care provision" for the purposes of Part 3. "Health care provision" means the provision of health care services as part of the comprehensive health service in England continued under section 1(1) of the National Health Service Act 2006: subsection 21(3). "Social care provision" means the provision made by a local authority in the exercise of its social services functions: subsection 21(4). However, by subsection 21(5), health care provision or social care provision which "educates or trains" a child or young person is to be treated as special educational provision for the purposes of Part 3 of the 2014 Act and specified in Section F. The operation of subsection 21(5) is addressed in further detail in Chapter 5.

Paragraph 9.69 of the SEND Code of Practice sets out in tabular format what to include in each section of the EHC plan, including Sections C, D, G, H1 and H2.

For social care provision in the plan, the duties on social care services derive from other legislation: principally the Children Act 1989, the Chronically Sick and Disabled Person Act 1970 and the Care Act 2014.

Subsection 2(4) of the 1970 Act provides that where a local authority has functions under Part 3 of the Children Act 1989 in relation to a disabled child and the child is ordinarily resident in its area, it must, in the exercise of those functions, make any arrangements within subsection 2(6) that it is satisfied it is necessary for it to make in order to meet the needs of the child. Arrangements under subsection 2(6) include the provision for the child or young person of practical assistance in their home; 'wireless', television, library or similar recreational facilities or assistance in obtaining them; lectures, games, outings or other recreational facilities outside their home or assistance in taking advantage of educational facilities; facilities for, or assistance in, travelling to and from their home for the purpose of participating in any services provided under arrangements made by the authority under Part 3 of the Children Act 1989 (or similar to services which could be provided under such arrangements); assistance in arranging for the carrying out of any works of adaptation in their home or any additional facilities designed to secure their greater safety, comfort or convenience; provision of meals for them; provision of a telephone and any special equipment necessary to enable them to use one.

The table at paragraph 9.69 of the SEND Code of Practice indicates that section H1 should include non-residential short breaks where the child as well as his or her parent will benefit from the short break. It also indicates that section H1 may include services to be provided for parent carers of disabled children, including following an assessment of their needs under sections 17ZD-17ZF of the 1989 Act. It also indicates that section H2 could include residential short breaks and services provided to children arising from their SEN but unrelated to a disability. It also states that H2 should include any provision secured through a social care direct payment.

Part 3 of the Children Act 1989 is headed 'Local Authority Support for Children and Families'. Under section 17, local authorities in England have a general duty to safeguard and promote the welfare of children within their area who are in need, and, so far as is consistent with that duty, to promote the upbringing of such children by their families, by providing a range and level of services appropriate to those children's needs. Subsection 17(10) defines a 'child in need' for purpose of Part 3 of the 1989 Act. This definition includes children who are "disabled" as defined by subsection 17(11). Part 1 of Schedule 2 of the 1989 Act sets out specific duties and powers which LAs have for the purpose principally of facilitating the discharge of their general duty under section 17.

Where a young person is over 18, the social care provision in the EHC plan will usually be met by adult services. The Care Act 2014 makes provision for local authorities to assess and meet eligible needs set out in a care and support plan. However, LAs have the power to continue to provide children's services past a young person's 18th birthday for as long as is deemed necessary. In addition, children's services must be maintained until a decision on adult provision is reached and where it is agreed that adult services will be provided. Young people can request an assessment for adult care in advance of their 18th birthday. Relevant statutory provisions include sections 58-59 of the Care Act 2014 and section 17ZH of the Children Act 1989.

If an EHC plan specifies health care provision, the "responsible commissioning body" must arrange the specified health care provision for the child or young person: subsection 42(3) of the 2014 Act. This means the body (or each body) that is under a duty to arrange health care provision of that kind in respect of the child or young person: subsection 42(4). If another commissioning body becomes responsible for the child or young person, the original responsible commissioning body must notify the new body of the change: regulation 16 of the 2014 Regulations. Where it is not practicable for the new commissioning body to arrange the health care provision specified in the EHC plan, it must request that the local authority makes an EHC needs assessment or reviews the EHC plan, and the local authority must comply with the request: regulation 16. By regulation 12(2), the health care provision specified in Section G of the EHC plan must be agreed by the responsible commissioning body.

By regulation 6 of the 2014 Regulations, where the local authority secures an EHC needs assessment for a child or young person, it must seek advice and information to include, *inter alia,* medical advice and information from a health care professional identified by the responsible commissioning body and advice and information in relation to social care. By regulation 8, where a local authority requests the co-operation of a body in securing an EHC needs assessment, that body must comply with such a request within 6 weeks of the date on which they receive it (unless it is impractical to do so for any of the reasons set out in regulation 8). By regulations 20 and 21, as part of a review of a child or young person's EHC plan, the invitees to the review meeting must include an officer of the LA who exercises the authority's social services functions in relation to children and young people with SEN, and a health care professional identified by the responsible commissioning body to provide advice about health care provision in relation to the child or young person. Advice and information about the child or young people should be obtained from the invitees in advance of the meeting.

This means that in most appeals brought under section 51 there should already exist some recent advice and information which relates to health care provision and social care provision, provided in the process of the EHC needs assessment or annual review. Assessments and care plans under the Children Act 1989 and under the Care Act 2014 may also form a part of the evidence in 'extended appeals'.

Under the Special Educational Needs and Disability (First-tier Tribunal Recommendations Power) Regulations 2017, parents and young people can request, and the Tribunal can make, non-binding recommendations about health and social care needs or provision as part of any type of appeal under section 51 of the 2014 Act except for appeals against the decision of a local authority not to secure an EHC needs assessment for the child or young person (i.e. appeals under section 51(2)(a)). These extended powers were tested under a 'National Trial' that started on 3 April 2018 and ran until 31 August 2021; since 1 September 2021, appeals which include health or social care aspects have been known as 'extended appeals'.

These provisions operate in the context of sections 25, 26 and 28 of the 2014 Act, which, broadly speaking, are intended to improve the way that services work together to provide support children and young people with educational, health and social care needs. Section 25 requires local authorities to carry out their functions under Part 3 in a way that promotes the integration of educational and training provision with health care provision and social care provision. Section 26 requires a LA and its "partner commissioning bodies" to make "joint commissioning arrangements" about the education, health and care provision to be secured for children and young people with SEN for whom it is responsible and for those in its area with disabilities. "Partner commissioning bodies" are defined in section 26 and include NHS England and integrated care boards. Section 28 requires a LA to co-operate with each of its "local partners" and each "local partner" to co-operate with the LA, in the exercise of the LA's functions under Part 3. "Local partners" are defined at subsection 28(2) and include NHS England, integrated care boards, NHS trusts or NHS foundation trusts and Local Health Boards. By subsection 28(3), LAs must make arrangements for ensuring co-operation between the officers of the LA who exercise the LA's functions relating to education or training and the officers of the LA who exercise the LA's social services functions for children or young people with special educational needs.

Chapter 2 of the SEND Code of Practice provides guidance on the information, advice and support which local authorities must provide for children, young people and parents, in relation to special educational needs, disability, health and social care.

Chapter 4 of the Code explains the statutory duties on local authorities to develop and publish a 'local offer' setting out the support they expect to be available for local children and young people with SEN or disabilities. Published information from the 'local offer' may often be relevant evidence in an 'extended appeal'.

Chapter 3 of the Code explains the duties which local authorities and their partner commissioning bodies have for developing joint arrangements for commissioning services to improve outcomes for children and young people aged 0 to 25 years who have SEN or disabilities. It provides substantial guidance in this respect, although it must now be read having regard to the changes made by the Health and Care Act 2022 which came into force on 1 July 2022. The 2022 Act has made substantial amendments to the National Health Service Act 2006 as well as to section 26 of the 2014 Act. The National Health Service Commissioning Board has been renamed NHS England and the establishment of integrated care board (ICBs) resulted in clinical commissioning groups (CCGs) being closed down.

The Special Educational Needs and Disability (First-tier Tribunal Recommendations Power) Regulations 2017 and 'extended appeals'

Regulation 8 provides that when a local authority notifies a child's parent or a young person of a decision in accordance with regulations 10(3), 14(2), 20(11), 21(10), 22(5), 25(2) or 31(3) of the Special Educational Needs and Disability Regulations 2014, the local authority must also notify the child's parent or the young person of the First-tier Tribunal's power to make recommendations under these Regulations.

Regulations 4 and 5 set out the powers the First-tier Tribunal to make recommendations in specified types of appeal.

In appeals under section 51(1)(b) – 'refusal to issue' appeals – the First-tier Tribunal has the power to recommend that health care needs, or health care needs of a particular kind, which relate to the child or young person's special educational needs, are specified in Section C of the EHC plan and that health care provision, or health care provision of a particular kind, is specified in Section G; it also has the power to recommend and that social care needs, or social care needs of a particular kind, which relate to the child or young person's SEN or to a disability are specified in Section D of the plan and that social care provision, or social care provision of a particular kind, is specified in Section H.

In appeals under section 51(2)(c), (d), (e) or (f) of the 2014 Act – Section 'B', 'F' or 'I' appeals, 'refusal to re-assess' appeals and 'ceasing to maintain' appeals – the First-tier Tribunal has the power to recommend amendments to Sections C, D, G and H of the EHC plan, including to specify needs or provision in those sections where no needs or provision have been specified.

If the First-tier Tribunal makes a recommendation in respect of health care needs or health care provision, it must send a copy of the recommendation to the responsible commissioning body (regulation 6(1)) and may also send a copy of its decision in the appeal (regulation 6(2)). "The responsible commissioning body" for this purpose means the body (or each body) that is under a duty to arrange health care provision of that kind in respect of the child or young person (or would be under that duty if the health care needs or health care provision recommended by Tribunal were specified in the child or young person's EHC plan): regulation 2. The responsible commissioning body must respond within 5 weeks beginning with the date of the recommendation to (a) the child's parent or the young person, and (b) the local authority that maintains the EHC plan, unless the Tribunal directs that a different time limit is to apply. The response must be in writing, state what steps, if any, the responsible commissioning body has decided to take following its consideration of the recommendation and give reasons for any decision not to follow the recommendation, or any part of it (regulations 6(3) to 6(4)). The LA must send a copy of this response to the Secretary of State within 1 week beginning with the date it was received (regulation 6(6)).

If the Tribunal makes a recommendation in respect of social care needs or social care provision, the local authority must respond to the child's parent or the young person within 5 weeks beginning with the date of the recommendation unless the Tribunal directs that a different time limit is to apply. Again, the response must be in writing, state what steps, if any, the LA has decided to take following its consideration of the recommendation and give reasons for any decision not to follow the recommendation, or any part of it: regulation 7. The LA must send a copy of the response to the Secretary of State within 1 week beginning with the date of its response to the child's parent or the young person.

The Guidance confirms that that the Tribunal will only make a recommendation about health and social care needs or provision which is related to a child or young person's learning difficulties or disabilities which result in them having SEN with the exception of any social care provision made under Section 2 of the Chronically Sick and Disabled Persons Act 1970. The Tribunal will not make decisions relating to conflicting clinical diagnosis from medical professionals concerning health needs or health provision.

The recommendations are non-binding, but the Guidance sets out that, should a local authority or responsible health commissioning body decide not to follow the recommendations of the Tribunal, parents and young people can use a range of alternative routes of redress, including complaining to the Ombudsman or seeking to have the decision judicially reviewed.

It would be rare for a responsible commissioning body to be joined as a party in an appeal. In *NHS West Berkshire Clinical Commissioning Group v The First-tier Tribunal (Health, Education and Social Care Chamber) (interested parties (1) AM; (2) MA; (3) Westminster City Council)* [2019] UKUT 44 (AAC) the CCG applied to be joined as a party to appeal proceedings before the First-tier Tribunal in order to make representations about the healthcare provision that could appropriately be made the subject of recommendation. Tribunal rejected the CCG's application, the CCG sought relief from the Upper Tribunal under its judicial review jurisdiction, and the Upper Tribunal dismissed that challenge. The background was a dispute between the CCG and the local authority. The CCG had assessed the child's eligibility for NHS Continuing Care and, in response to the NHS Continuing Care eligibility decision, the LA took the view that the CCG were responsible for all aspects of the child's care and support requirements including, it seemed, any support of an educational or training nature, and decided to cease to maintain the child's EHC plan. The Upper Tribunal's reasons in *NHS West Berkshire CCG* make clear that a recommendation of the First-tier Tribunal in an extended appeal is not akin to an order under regulation 43 of the 2014 Regulations. Mitchell J stated, at [100], that the CCG's interests were not those of a person whose substantive rights and obligations were liable to be determined by the Tribunal. The First-tier Tribunal had taken case management steps to appraise itself of the CCG position which permitted the CCG to set out its views, and arrangements were made for a CCG witness to attend the final hearing. Since the Tribunal had no power to fix the CCG with an obligation to provide any support for the child, the CCG was treated fairly.

The usual process in an extended appeal is that the appellant must indicate in the appeal form whether they are seeking health and/or social care recommendations. The grounds of appeal will then be considered by a First-tier Tribunal judge who will identify the issues in the appeal and make directions for the local authority to provide evidence from the health and social care bodies in response to the issues raised, within the timeframe specified in the directions, and the parties can seek permission to bring additional witnesses to the hearing to address the health and/or social care issues. Health and LA social care commissioners must respond to any request for information and evidence from the Tribunal within the timeframe specified and, if required, the health and LA social care commissioners must send a witness from the health and/or social care bodies to attend the hearing to give oral evidence.

The Guidance sets out that evidence from health and social care professionals should clearly specify a child or young person's health or social care needs and the provision required to meet each of those needs. It should also identify the outcomes expected if that provision is put into place over a period of time. This means that the evidence must be clear as to what needs a child or young person has and in quantifying and qualifying what provision they require, including who will deliver that provision, when, how often, for how long and the arrangements that should be in place to monitor its effectiveness.

However, in *VS and RS v Hampshire County Council* [2021] UKUT 187 (AAC), the Upper Tribunal considered the level of 'specificity' that was required in relation to health and social care recommendations. Authorities relating to specificity of special educational provision in Section F cannot simply be read across to apply to the exercise of the recommendations power where Sections C, D, G and H are concerned.

When a recommendation is specific, that will assist those concerned with delivering provision to the child or young person in understanding what the First-tier Tribunal had in mind. The more specific that the First-tier Tribunal can be, the more specific the relevant health or social care body is likely to have to be in providing its reasoned response to the recommendation if their response is to be legally adequate. However, given the nature of the power, the Tribunal needs to be free to make constructive recommendations in relation to health and social care provision. How specific it feels it can be is essentially a matter for the Tribunal taking into account all relevant factors. *VS and RS v Hampshire County Council* is another Upper Tribunal decision which confirms that there is a qualitative difference between what the First-tier Tribunal is empowered to do in relation to educational provision, where its decisions may create an enforceable right, and its power to make recommendations under the 2017 Regulations in the same appeal.

Under The Tribunal Procedure (First-tier Tribunal) (Health, Education and Social Care Chamber) Rules 2008 Rules, the Tribunal has extensive powers to direct the production of evidence by the parties and by third parties where it considers it necessary, and powers to direct that existing evidence be supplemented or its adequacy improved. The Tribunal can also issue witness summonses to require the attendance of witnesses who have indicated to the parties that they will not attend the hearing voluntarily.

CHAPTER TEN

THE FIRST-TIER TRIBUNAL IN SPECIAL EDUCATIONAL NEEDS CASES – PRACTICE AND PROCEDURE

Following the creation of the unified tribunal system under the Tribunals, Courts and Enforcement Act 2007, the jurisdiction of the Special Educational Needs and Disability Tribunal ("SENDIST") was transferred to the Health, Education and Social Care Chamber of the First-tier Tribunal. The Tribunal is now referred to as the First-tier Tribunal (Special Educational Needs and Disability) or the 'SEND Tribunal'.

Section 51(1) of the Children and Families Act 2014 provides that "a child's parent or a young person" may appeal to the First-tier Tribunal against the matters set out in subsection 51(2), subject to section 55 (mediation). The matters set out in section 51(2) are explained in this book in Chapters 2 to 8. Mediation is explained further in this Chapter, below.

LB Bromley v SENT [1999] ELR 260 established the key principle that when deciding an appeal, the Tribunal "stands in the LEA's shoes, re-evaluating the available information in order if necessary to recast the statement." When the Tribunal comes to make its decision, it is bound at that stage to look at the overall picture as to the particular special needs of the child *at that time*; it is not for the Tribunal simply to address the issues as at the stage when the EHC plan is drawn or when the appellant lodges the appeal: see *Wilkin v Goldthorpe (Chair of the SEN Tribunal)* CO/1251/97; *Hammersmith & Fulham LBC v L & F* [2015] UKUT 523 (AAC) at [35]; *Gloucestershire CC v EH (SEN)* [2017] UKUT 85 (AAC) at [47]. In *DH & GH v Staffordshire* CC [2018] UKUT 49 (AAC) at [19] the Upper Tribunal stated:

> "This appeal is sometimes called a general appeal. This means that the issue for the tribunal is whether, on the evidence and submissions before it, the local authority came to the correct conclusions on matters of fact, law and judgment. The tribunal is free to form its own view on any matters covered by the decision. But the extent of its powers and duties vary. In some types of case the tribunal is limited to considering the circumstances obtaining at the date of the decision under appeal, whereas in other types of case the tribunal has to consider the circumstances obtaining at the date of the hearing. Special education needs appeals are dealt with as at the date of the hearing: *Gloucestershire County Council v EH [2017] ELR 193* at [47]. Again, in some types of case the tribunal will undertake the whole process afresh, whereas in other types of case the issues are narrower. Special educational needs appeals regularly limit the issues to those identified as being in dispute in a working document produced by the parties."

Subject to the provisions of the Tribunals, Courts and Enforcement Act 2007 and any other enactment, the First-tier Tribunal may regulate its own procedure. The relevant procedure rules are The Tribunal Procedure (First-tier Tribunal) (Health, Education and Social Care Chamber) Rules 2008 ("the Procedure Rules"). In addition, section 23 of the 2007 Act gives the Senior President of Tribunals and a Chamber President a power to make practice directions. The President of the Health, Education and Social Care Chamber issued a practice direction on 20 April 2021 which applies to special educational needs cases (as defined at rule 1(3) of the Procedure Rules). The Procedure Rules, forms and other guidance is available on the SEND Tribunal's website.

Regulations 43 of the Special Educational Needs and Disability Regulations 2014 makes provision for the powers of the First-tier Tribunal before or when determining any appeal. Regulation 44 deals with compliance with the orders of the First-tier Tribunal. Regulation 45 makes provision for unopposed appeals, where the local authority notifies the First-tier Tribunal that it will not oppose the appeal before it submits a response. These regulations are considered further in Chapters 2-8 of this book.

The First-tier Tribunal's practice and procedure in relation to Part 5 of the Procedure Rules, which deals with correcting, setting aside, reviewing and appealing First-tier Tribunal decisions, is addressed in Chapter 11.

'Parent', 'child' and 'young person'

Section 576 of the 1996 Act provides that "parent", in relation to a child or young person, includes any person (a) who is not a parent of his but who has parental responsibility for him, or (b) who has care of him. In this context "parental responsibility" has the same meaning as in the Children Act 1989, section 3, and, in determining for these purposes whether an individual has care of a child or young person, any absence of the child or young person at a hospital or boarding school and any other temporary absence must be disregarded. By section 579 of the 1996 Act, "child" means a person who is not over compulsory school age. By section 83 of the 2014 Act, "young person" means a person over compulsory school age but under 25. The definition of compulsory school age is found in section 8 of the 1996 Act together with the Education (School Leaving Date) Order 1997, 1997/1970 and the Education (Start of Compulsory School Age) Order 1998, SI 1998/1607, made under section 8(4) and section 579. A child begins to be of compulsory school age on 31 December, 31 March or 31 August following their fifth birthday, whichever comes first; if their fifth birthday is on one of those dates then they reach compulsory school age on that date. A child ceases to be of compulsory school age on the last Friday in June if they have reached the age of 16 by that date or will have reached it before the beginning of the next school year i.e. by the start of the next school term to begin after July.

Capacity

Where a young person lacks capacity to bring an appeal, provision is made by section 80 of the 2014 Act and regulation 64 of the 2014 Regulations. The Upper Tribunal gave detailed guidance on how this operates in *Buckinghamshire County Council v SJ* [2016] UKUT 0254 (AAC) at [8-20] and in *London Borough of Hillingdon v WW* (SEN) [2016] UKUT 253 (AAC) at [6-19].

Section 80 of the 2014 Act adopts the meaning of lacking capacity that applies in the Mental Health Act 2005. Capacity depends on the matter in respect of which a decision has to be made: section 2(1) of the 2005 Act. Therefore, a young person may *have* capacity in respect of bringing an appeal but not in respect of other decisions that have to be made in the course of the proceedings; equally, they may *lack* capacity to bring an appeal but *have* capacity to make other decisions in the course of the proceedings. A person is presumed to have capacity until shown otherwise and then only after all practical steps have been taken without success to help them make a decision: section 1(2) and (3) of 2005 Act.

Whether a young person has capacity to bring an appeal is a matter of fact for the First-tier Tribunal to decide. By section 2(4) of the 2005 Act, the question must be decided on the balance of probabilities.

Rule 2(4) of the Procedure Rules requires parties to co-operate with the Tribunal, which may involve drawing to the Tribunal's attention any issue relating to a young person's capacity to bring an appeal and providing the Tribunal with any evidence it needs to resolve the issue. If an issue arises, the most efficient way to resolve it may be to deal with it as a preliminary issue under rule 5(3)(e).

Young people who <u>have</u> capacity may appoint someone to help and advocate for them; that person could be a parent or someone with some form of professional position. However, the appeal is brought by the young person.

The term 'representative' is used in a different sense when the young person lacks capacity. Section 80 makes provision for references to a young person to be read as references to, or as including references to, a "representative" of the young person or the young person's parent, where a young person lacks capacity at the relevant time. The term "representative" is not used here in the sense of an advocate in proceedings: it refers to a person who acts for someone who lacks capacity. It is defined in section 80(6) and covers a Court of Protection deputy, a donee of a lasting power of attorney and an attorney of an enduring power of attorney. Regulation 64 introduces the concept of an "alternative person". The starting point is that the young person's "representative" in the section 80 sense is the "alternative person": regulation 64(2)(a). If the young person does not have a "representative" in the section 80 sense, the "alternative person" means the young person's parent: regulation 64(2)(b). The effect of this for the purposes of section 51 is that the reference to young person is read as a reference to the alternative person: regulation 64(1)(b) and Part 2 of Schedule 3. The result is that an appeal under section 51 is brought by the alternative person. An alternative person who is a representative in the section 80 sense may act on their own or use the services of a representative in the advocacy sense.

There is guidance on mental capacity in Annex 1 to the SEND Code of Practice, where the second paragraph states, 'in most cases where a young person lack capacity, decisions will be taken on their behalf by their parent.' Strictly, decisions are not taken by the parent on the young person's behalf: rather, they are taken by the parent in their capacity as the alternative person and in the young person's best interests.

There is an extra consideration for a young person who is aged 16 or 17. These persons are still children for the purposes of the Children Act 1989 and their parents retain parental responsibility. Section 27(1)(g) of the 2005 Act preserves that responsibility, except for property matters. Regulation 65 of the 2014 Regulations provides that regulation 64 applies despite section 27, but that does not deprive the parents of their responsibility generally.

If a young person's capacity changes during the course of proceedings, the Tribunal may substitute another party as appellant: rule 9 of the Procedure Rules. A young person who was the appellant before the First-tier Tribunal but lacks capacity before the Upper Tribunal will nevertheless be a party before the Upper Tribunal (see the definition of 'respondent' in rule 1(3) of the Upper Tribunal's rules) until a substitution is made under rule 9 of the Upper Tribunal's rules.

In *Buckinghamshire County Council v SJ* [2016] UKUT 0254 at [18] and *London Borough of Hillingdon v WW* (SEN) [2016] UKUT 253 (AAC) at [17] Jacobs J considered whether the provisions of the 2014 Act or Regulations involved any 'deprivation of liberty' for the purposes of the 2005 Act or an infringement of the young person's Convention rights. He considered *CB v London Borough of Merton and the Special Educational Needs Tribunal* [2002] ELR 441 in which the Tribunal had named a residential school against the parents' wishes. Sullivan J, at [20], rejected the argument that this infringed the child's Article 8 rights since the Tribunal had not ordered the child to attend the school: that was a matter for the local authority if it decided to serve a school attendance order and any challenge would then relate to that order, not the Tribunal's decision to name the school. Jacobs J also considered *X v County Council v DW* [2005] EWHC 162 (Fam) in which Munby J said, at [20], that the decision of a Tribunal on placement did not oblige a parent to accept that decision and they were free to make other arrangements. It would follow that a Tribunal's decision to name a residential placement in the case of a young person who lacks capacity does not in itself involve any 'deprivation of liberty' for the purposes of the 2005 Act or any infringement of the young person's Convention rights, but such issues could arise subsequently in relation to the young person's actual attendance there. Further consideration of such issues and the jurisdiction of the Court of Protection falls outside the scope of this book.

Where parents are acting separately or disagree

Section 51 affords a right of appeal to "a" parent. The application for appeal form, Form SEND 35 provides for up to two people to make the appeal, so two parents can be named as appellants in the same appeal. Consistent with the 20 April 2021 practice direction, Form SEND35 requires the appellant to give the name and contact details of any other person or organisation who shares parental responsibility for the child or has been appointed as a deputy by the Court of Protection for a young person and confirm that the appellant has notified them of the appeal. The form gives the appellant an opportunity, if they believe that person or organisation should not receive details of the appeal, to explain why. The form also requires the appellant to provide the details of any order made by any other court or tribunal order concerning the child or young person.

The First-tier Tribunal can join others with a right of appeal to proceedings that are under way "as respondent". The position such a person adopts in relation to the substantive issues in the appeal will not be determined by the label of "respondent" they are given: *JW v Kent CC* (SEN) [2017] UKUT 281 (AAC) at [13]. Rule 9 of the Procedure Rules provides that the Tribunal may give a direction substituting a party or adding a person to the proceedings as a respondent, but it does not provide for a party to be added to the proceedings as an applicant. Consequently a "parent" can be joined as a "respondent" to an appeal, even if they do *not* disagree with the parent who is the appellant.

In practice, where another person who shares parental responsibility for the child has been identified on the application for appeal form, a Tribunal is likely to manage the case by directing that person to indicate to the appellant and to the Tribunal whether they are content to have their views submitted to the Tribunal in writing or whether they want to play an active role in the appeal by either applying to be joined as a respondent or requesting that the local authority call them (or if the person is an organisation, an individual from the organisation) to give evidence as a witness at the hearing.

The Upper Tribunal in *S-G v Denbighshire County Council and B* (SEN): [2016] UKUT 460 (AAC) provided some guidance on the law relating to placement, where two parents did not agree on the school their child should attend (see further in Chapter 6 on 'Section I' appeals).

The role of the Tribunal and the overriding objective of the Procedure Rules

Rule 2 of the Procedure Rules states that the overriding objective of the Rules is to enable the Tribunal to deal with cases fairly and justly which includes: (a) dealing with the case in ways which are proportionate to the importance of the case, the complexity of the issues, the anticipated costs and the resources of the parties; (b) avoiding unnecessary formality and seeking flexibility in the proceedings; (c) ensuring, so far as practicable, that the parties are able to participate fully in the proceedings; (d) using any special expertise of the Tribunal effectively; and (e) avoiding delay, so far as compatible with proper consideration of the issues.

The Tribunal must seek to give effect to the overriding objective when it exercises any power under the Procedure Rules or interprets any rule or practice direction (as defined by section 23 of the Tribunals, Courts and Enforcement Act 2007): rule 2(3). In addition, parties must help the Tribunal to further the overriding objective; and co-operate with the Tribunal generally: rule 2(4).

Starting an appeal, mediation, and time limits

A parent or young person may only appeal to the First-tier Tribunal under section 51 of the 2014 Act if a mediation advisor has issued a certificate to him or her under subsections 55(4) or 55(5): section 55(3). The exception to this requirement is where the appeal <u>only</u> concerns the school or other institution named the EHC plan, the type of school or other institution specified the plan, or the fact that the plan does not name a school or other institution (i.e. the appeal relates to Section I <u>only</u>): subsection 55(2).

Where a parent or young person is required to obtain a mediation certificate, they must contact the mediation adviser within 2 months after written notice of the local authority's decision was sent and inform the mediation adviser that they wish to appeal and inform the mediation adviser whether they wish to pursue mediation: regulation 33 of the 2014 Regulations. However, by regulation 34(3), a parent or young person may seek leave to appeal to the First-tier Tribunal not withstanding that they are required to obtain a mediation certificate and a mediation adviser has not issued a certificate to them, where the parent or young person has failed to comply with regulation 33 and the time for doing so has elapsed. The process for doing so is addressed by rule 19 of the Procedure Rules.

Sections 52 to 56 of the 2014 Act, regulations 32 to 42 of the 2014 Regulations and paragraphs 11.13 to 11.38 of the SEND Code of Practice 2015 deal further with mediation.

If rule 19 (application for leave, where leave is required by virtue of regulation 34(3) of the 2014 Regulations) does not apply, then, by rule 20(1)(c) of the Procedure Rules, an applicant must start proceedings before the Tribunal by sending or delivering an application notice to the Tribunal so that it is received within 2 months after written notice of the decision being challenged was sent to the applicant; or within 1 month from the date of issue of the mediation certificate if that date would be a later date. Under rule 5(3)(a) the Tribunal has a power to extend time. By rule 12(3)(a), if the time for starting proceedings under rule 20 ends on a day from 25th December to 1st January inclusive, or on any day in August, the application notice is provided in time if it is provided to the Tribunal on the first working day after 1st January or 31st August.

By rule 20(4)(a), if the applicant provides the application notice after the expiry of the time limit or any extension of time, the application notice must include a request for an extension of time and the reason why the application notice was not provided in time.

Unless the Tribunal extends time for the application notice under rule 5(3)(a), the Tribunal must not admit the application notice: rule 20(4)(b). In *CM v Surrey CC* (SEN) [2014] UKUT 4 (AAC) the Upper

Tribunal at [15-17] considered the case law and principles relevant to the exercise of the Tribunal's discretion in this regard. The power in rule 5(3)(a) is unfettered; as such it has to be exercised judicially and in accordance with the overriding objective in rule 2. Each case should be considered on its own facts. A range of considerations which are likely, and very often highly likely, to be relevant are the length of the delay, the reasons for the delay, the chances of the appeal succeeding if the application is granted, and the degree of prejudice to the respondent if the application is granted. Other factors, such as the impact on other users of the tribunal system, may also need to be taken into account. If the delay is short and readily excusable, it may well be that the merits of the case may have little, if any, significance, but in other cases the merits (or rather the lack thereof) may assume greater importance. The longer the delay, the stronger the underlying case may need to be to justify extending time. However, a detailed examination of the merits is not to be expected as the decision is a procedural or interlocutory one. The adequacy of the explanation for the late appeal/application is an important consideration under rule 5(3)(a) but it is only the beginning of the enquiry. The weight to be attached to all the various factors is a matter for the Tribunal, depending on all the circumstances.

Paragraphs 15 and 16 of the 20 April 2021 practice direction note that regulations 5(3), 10(3), 14(2), 20(11), 21(10), 22(5), 25(2) and 31(3) of the 2014 regulations all set out requirements for the local authority to notify the child's parent or the young person of their right to appeal to the Tribunal and the time limit in which to do so, and in relation to dispute resolution arrangements, and the Tribunal may have regard to any failure by the LA in this regard when considering whether to extend time where the application notice was not provided within the time limit set out in rule 20(1)(c).

Rule 20(2) states that the application notice must be signed by the applicant (only a legal representative may sign the application notice on the applicant's behalf (rule 11(3)(b)) and sets out the information it must contain. The practice direction also sets out information which the application notice must also contain. In practice the Tribunal form, currently Form SEND35, or SEND35a (for 'refusal to assess' appeals), should set out the information which the applicant should provide. In *KD v Essex CC* [2018] UKUT 147 at [2-3] the Upper Tribunal held that a failure to comply with the requirements of rule 20(2) does not render a purported application notice invalid and the Tribunal is required to admit the application notice and register the appeal to which it relates. However, some purported application notices could be so defectively drafted, or lacking in specifics, that they cannot properly be construed as disclosing an intention to start proceedings and, in such cases, there is no application notice as a matter of law.

Rule 20(3) states that the applicant must send with the application notice a copy of any written record of the decision under challenge and any statement of reasons for that decision which the applicant has or can reasonably obtain, and, in cases to which section 55(3) of the 2014 Act applies (cases in which an appeal may be made only if a mediation certificate has been issued), a copy of the mediation certificate.

Calculating time for compliance with rules, practice directions or directions, parties' representatives, and sending and delivery of documents

By rule 12(1), the default position is that any act required by the Procedure Rules, a practice direction or a direction to be done on or by a particular day must be done by 5pm on that day. If the time specified by the Procedure Rules, a practice direction or a direction for doing any act ends on a day other than a working day, the act is done in time if it is done on the next working day: rule 12(2). In SEN cases specifically, the days from 25th December to 1st January inclusive and any day in August must not be counted when calculating the time by which any other act must be done: rule 12(3)(b). However, this does not apply where the Tribunal directs that an act must be done by or on a specified date: rule 12(4).

Rule 11 makes provision for a party to appoint a representative (whether a legal representative or not) to represent them in the proceedings. At a hearing a party may be accompanied by another person whose name and address has not been notified as their representative under rule 11(2) but who, with the permission of the Tribunal, may act as a representative or otherwise assist in presenting the party's case at the hearing.

Rule 13 deals with sending and delivery of documents to the Tribunal and the parties or their representatives. The Tribunal provides an address for contact on its website including an email address.

Case directions, the local authority's response to the appeal, and the 'working document'

The Tribunal will send a copy of the application notice and accompanying documents to the respondent local authority with case directions issued under rule 5 of the Procedure Rules which will be sent to both parties.

Rule 21(c) of the Procedure Rules provides that in a SEN case, when a respondent receives a copy of the application notice, the respondent must send or deliver to the Tribunal a response so that it is received within 30 working days after the respondent received the application notice. In practice, the Tribunal's case directions will set out when the local authority must send its response to the applicant and to the Tribunal.

Rule 21(2) sets out what the response must include. The response must include, *inter alia*, the views of the child about the issues raised by the proceedings, or the reason why the local authority has not ascertained those views: rule 21(2)(e). In practice, the Tribunal's requirements as to what the respondent local authority must include in the response will be set out in the case directions sent to the parties. There is also guidance on the Tribunal website for LAs on preparing a SEND tribunal case which includes guidance on what to include in the response. The response may include a statement as to whether the respondent would be content for the case to be dealt with without a hearing if the Tribunal considers it appropriate: rule 21(3).

Paragraph 12 of the 20 April 2021 practice direction also requires that if the appeal relates to the contents of an EHC plan and the local authority does not resist the appeal (or withdraws its opposition to the appeal) it must send a final amended plan incorporating the amendments to the plan which it agrees to make.

If the respondent provides the response to the Tribunal later than the time required or by any extension of time under rule 5(3)(a) – the Tribunal's power to extend time – the response must include a request for an extension of time and the reason why the response was not provided in time: rule 21(4).

The respondent must send or deliver a copy of the response and any accompanying documents to each other party at the same time as it provides the response to the Tribunal: rule 21(5).

The 'working document'

If the appeal relates to the content of an existing EHC plan, the case directions will probably also direct the local authority to send an electronic copy of the EHC plan to the applicant in an editable format to start the 'working document process'.

The Tribunal has published guidance relating to the 'working document': currently SEND23.

The 'working document' is a copy of the final EHC plan, on which both parties will have worked to show the changes to the wording of the EHC plan that they want or can agree, as well as those issues which the Tribunal must decide on the day of the final hearing. Usually, because the local authority has prepared the final EHC plan electronically, they prepare the first draft, after they have seen the Notice of Appeal. The case directions may specifically direct the LA to send the first 'draft' to the applicant indicating the LA's proposed amendments, if any. The Tribunal recommends a standard 'key' to the document which will show each party's position. For example, the original EHC plan will be in normal type, the LA's proposed amendments will be in italic type and the LA's proposed deletions will be shown in italic type, struck through. The applicant can then amend it to show, using the key, their proposed amendments and deletions and the changes proposed by the LA which they are prepared to agree.

The case directions will normally direct that local authority send the final version of the working document to the applicant and Tribunal so that it is received at least 10 working days before the hearing. The SEND23 guidance stresses that the Tribunal only needs the last copy of the document and that the parties should not send it every copy prepared in the course of negotiations. In practice, it is not uncommon for negotiations to continue into the 10 days before the final hearing and further versions of the working document are produced. This means the Tribunal Judge will often seek to confirm with the parties at the outset of the hearing that the Tribunal has the version of the document which is the final version.

The role of the local authority in the proceedings

Although the proceedings are in part adversarial because the local authority will be responding to the parent's (or young person's) appeal, its role as a public body at such a hearing is to assist the Tribunal by making all relevant information available; its role is not to provide only so much information as will assist its own case: *JF v Croydon LBC* [2006] EWHC 2368 at [11]. In *A J v. London Borough of Croydon* [2020] UKUT 246 (AAC) the Upper Tribunal held, at [130] and [133]: "That is not to require the authority to embark on an evidence gathering exercise willy-nilly and regardless of context, but one dependent on the facts of the individual case to provide all such information as is *relevant* to the decision under appeal." In *AC v LB Richmond on Thames* [2020] UKUT 380 (AAC) the Upper Tribunal held that the LA should supply any material which it thinks is likely to assist the Tribunal in reaching a just decision on the appeal before it, and where the LA is in doubt about whether such material in its possession would assist in this way, it should "play safe" and produce it: at [4] and [17].

There is guidance for local authorities on the Tribunal website on preparing a SEND tribunal case.

Both parties must help the Tribunal to further the overriding objective of the Procedure Rules and co-operate with the Tribunal generally: rule 2(4).

Other case directions

The case directions sent to both parties may also set out specific information which the parties, or a specified party, must provide. For example, in a 'Section I' appeal, the case directions will often direct the LA, or the applicant, to provide specific information such as the Ofsted report for the school they are asking the Tribunal to name. In 'extended appeals', the case directions are likely to be more extensive, identifying the issues in the extended appeal and specifying health or social care information which the LA must provide.

The case directions will usually indicate a date by which 'further evidence' may be submitted, after which no further evidence will be accepted without express permission of the Tribunal.

The case directions will usually also direct the local authority to prepare a bundle for the final hearing consisting of all the documents submitted by the applicant and the LA by the further evidence deadline, and the date by which it must be sent to the Tribunal and the other party. The Tribunal has published guidance in relation to producing the bundle: currently SEND40.

Notice of hearings, attendance at the hearing and 'Attendance Forms'

The case directions will usually also indicate the date of the final hearing. By rule 25, the Tribunal must give each party entitled to attend a hearing reasonable notice of the time and place of the hearing (including any adjourned or postponed hearing) and any changes to the time and place of the hearing; the period of notice under rule 25(1) must be at least 14 days, except that the Tribunal may give shorter notice with the parties' consent or in urgent or exceptional circumstances. Since the Covid-19 pandemic it has become very usual practice for hearings to be held 'remotely' using video.

Hearings in SEN cases must be held in private unless the Tribunal considers that it is in the interests of justice for a hearing to be held in public: rule 26(2). In practice a public hearing would be very rare. The Tribunal may determine who is permitted to attend the hearing or part of the hearing which is to be held in private: rule 26(4). However, rule 24 states that each party is entitled to attend a hearing and that, in a SEN case brought by a parent of a child, the child is entitled to attend a hearing and the Tribunal may permit the child to give evidence and to address the Tribunal.

This rule is subject to rule 26(5) which gives the Tribunal powers to exclude a person from a hearing in specified circumstances. The Tribunal may also give a direction excluding a witness from a hearing until that witness gives evidence: rule 26(6). In an appeal brought by a parent of a child or by a young person who lacks capacity to conduct their case, the Tribunal may exclude the child or young person from the hearing if the Tribunal considers that their presence would be adverse to their interests: rule 26(5)(e). The circumstances in which a Tribunal invokes rule 26(5) or 26(6) to exclude a person from a hearing do not commonly arise.

In practice it is quite usual for children or young people, including those who have capacity to conduct their own case, not to attend hearings, although they would be entitled to do so.

The 20 April 2021 practice direction states that the following persons (in addition to the party and the child or young person) will normally be entitled to attend the final hearing, or part of it unless the Tribunal determines otherwise or they are excluded under rule 26(5) or (6): the party's representative and witnesses; any other person the party has informed the Tribunal they wish to attend the hearing unless the Tribunal has determined that any such person should not attend the hearing and has notified that party accordingly; a parent of the child who is not a party to the application; the Chamber President and any judge or other member of the First-tier Tribunal (when not sitting as a member of the Tribunal); a person undergoing training as a judge or other member of the First-tier Tribunal or as a member of staff; a person acting under the supervision of the Chamber President in the training or supervision of a member of staff; an interpreter.

The case directions will usually indicate dates by which the parties must submit their 'Attendance Forms' on which they must indicate who will be attending the hearing. The Attendance Form will usually indicate that if a party wishes to call more than three witnesses (or more than five witnesses in an extended appeal), they must apply for the Tribunal's permission. The Attendance Form for the local authority will usually indicate just one representative for the LA. This means that if the LA will have legal representation at the hearing but has a reason why an officer of the LA, who is not attending as a witness, should also attend, it should seek the Tribunal's permission. The Tribunal may give permission for a person to attend the hearing as an observer for a variety of reasons. The Attendance Form for the parents or young person will usually indicate that they, in addition to any representative, may attend the hearing.

The Tribunal's case management powers and 'requests for change'

The Tribunal has a wide range of general case management powers which are set out in the Procedure Rules at rule 5. It may give a direction in relation to the conduct or disposal of proceedings at any time, including a direction amending, suspending or setting aside an earlier direction: rule 5(2). Rule 5(3) sets out particular powers which do not restrict the general powers in rule 5. These are to: extend or shorten the time for complying with any rule, practice direction or direction, unless such extension or shortening would conflict with a provision of another enactment containing a time limit; consolidate or hear together two or more sets of proceedings or parts of proceedings raising common issues, or treat a case as a lead case; permit or require a party to amend a document; permit or require a party or another person to provide documents, information or submissions to the Tribunal or a party; deal with an issue in the proceedings as a preliminary issue; hold a hearing to consider any matter, including a case management issue; decide the form of any hearing; adjourn or postpone a hearing; require a party to produce a bundle for a hearing; stay proceedings; transfer proceedings to another court or tribunal if that other court or tribunal has jurisdiction in relation to the proceedings and because of a change of circumstances since the proceedings were started, the Tribunal no longer has jurisdiction in relation to the proceedings or the Tribunal considers that the other court or tribunal is a more appropriate forum for the determination of the case; suspend the effect of its own decision pending the determination by the Tribunal or the Upper Tribunal of an application for permission to appeal against, and any appeal or review of, that decision.

By rule 6(1), the Tribunal may give a direction on the application of one or more of the parties or on its own initiative. Rule 6 (2)(a) and (3) sets out the procedure for applying for directions. An application for a direction may be made by sending or delivering a written application to the Tribunal and must include the reason for making that application. A 'request for change' form is provided on the Tribunal website for this purpose: currently SEND7. This stipulates, 'Before submitting the request you must have consulted the other party (if you have not done so your request will be returned to you)'. In addition, parties may apply for directions orally during the course of a hearing: rule 6(2)(b). If the Tribunal makes a direction, it must send written notice of it to every party and to any other person affected by it, unless it considers that there is a good reason not to: rule 6(4). If a party or any other person given notice of a direction wishes to challenge it, they may do so by applying for another direction which amends, suspends or sets aside the first direction: rule 6(5).

Rule 7 sets out the effect of non-compliance with any requirement in the Procedure Rules, a practice direction or a direction. Non-compliance does not of itself render void the proceedings or any step taken in the proceedings. If a party has failed to comply, the Tribunal may take such action as it considers just, which may include waiving the requirement, requiring the failure to be remedied, exercising its power under rule 8 (striking out a party's case) or restricting a party's participation in the proceedings. Rule 12(3) sets out circumstances in which the Tribunal may ask the Upper Tribunal to exercise powers it has under section 25 of the 2007 Act akin to those of the High Court, which relate to the attendance and examination of witnesses and the production and inspection of documents. Sections 51(6) and (7) of the 2014 Act provides that a person commits an offence (liable on summary conviction to a fine not exceeding level 3 on the standard scale) if without reasonable excuse that person fails to comply with any requirement in respect of the discovery or inspection of documents, or to attend to give evidence and produce documents, where that requirement is imposed by Tribunal Procedure Rules in relation to an appeal under section 51 of the 2014 Act.

The Tribunal has a number of specific case management powers set out in other rules: to strike out a party's case (rule 8), to substitute a party or add a respondent (rule 9); to make an order for costs (rule 10), to make an order prohibiting the disclosure or publication of— specified documents or information relating to the proceedings or any matter likely to lead members of the public to identify any person whom the Tribunal considers should not be identified (rule 14); to make directions regarding evidence or submissions that it requires (rule 15); to summons witnesses or order a person to answer questions or produce documents (rule 16).

Prohibiting disclosure and publication

Rule 14 affords the Tribunal power to make a variety of orders prohibiting the disclosure or publication of documents or information, including any matter likely to lead members of the public to identify any person whom the Tribunal considers should not be identified. It is usual practice for the Tribunal to make orders prohibiting disclosure or publication of any matter likely to lead members of the public to identify the child or young person who is the subject of a SEN appeal without the permission of a judge of the Tribunal. In *Re a Teacher (Rule 14 Order)*

[2023] UKUT 39 (AAC) the Upper Tribunal (Ward J) considered how far an order under rule 14 of the Upper Tribunal's rules extends.

Striking out and barring

Rule 8 deals with striking out proceedings, or parts of proceedings, and barring the respondent from taking further part in the proceedings.

Rule 8(2) provides that the proceedings, or the appropriate part of them, will automatically be struck out if the applicant has failed to comply with a direction that stated that failure by the applicant to comply with the direction would lead to the striking out of the proceedings or that part of them. By rule 8(4)(a), the Tribunal may strike out the whole or a part of the proceedings if the applicant has failed to comply with a direction which stated that failure by the applicant to comply with the direction could lead to the striking out of the proceedings or part of them. It may do so under rule 8(4)(a) without first giving the applicant an opportunity to make representations in relation to the proposed striking out. However, where proceedings have been struck out under rule 8(2) or rule 8(4)(a) then, under rule 8(6), the applicant may apply for the proceedings, or part of them, to be reinstated. Such application must be made in writing and received by the Tribunal within 28 days after the date on which the Tribunal sent notification of the striking out to that party: rule 8(7).

By rule 8(3), the Tribunal must strike out the whole or a part of the proceedings if the Tribunal does not have jurisdiction in relation to the proceedings or that part of them and does not exercise its power under rule 5(3)(k)(i) in relation to the proceedings or that part of them. Rule 5(3)(k)(i) provides a power to transfer proceedings to another court or tribunal if that other court or tribunal has jurisdiction in relation to the proceedings and, because of a change of circumstances since the proceedings were started, the Tribunal no longer has jurisdiction in relation to the proceedings.

By rules 8(4)(b) and 8(4)(c), the Tribunal may strike out the whole or a part of the proceedings if the applicant has failed to co-operate with the Tribunal to such an extent that the Tribunal cannot deal with the proceedings fairly and justly or the Tribunal considers there is no reasonable prospect of the applicant's case, or part of it, succeeding. By rule 8(5), the Tribunal may not strike out the whole or a part of the proceedings under rule 8(3) or 8(4)(b) or (c) without first giving the applicant an opportunity to make representations in relation to the proposed striking out.

By rule 8(8), rule 8 applies to a respondent as it applies to an applicant except that a reference to the striking out of the proceedings is to be read as a reference to the barring of the respondent from taking further part in the proceedings; and a reference to an application for the reinstatement of proceedings which have been struck out is to be read as a reference to an application for the lifting of the bar on the respondent from taking further part in the proceedings.

If a respondent has been barred from taking further part in proceedings under rule 8 and that bar has not been lifted, the effect is that Tribunal need not consider any response or other submission made by that respondent and may summarily determine any or all issues against that respondent: rule 8(9).

In *Royal Borough of Kensington & Chelsea* v MJ [2017] UKUT 102 (AAC) the conditions of a previous "unless" order were triggered so that the respondent local authority was barred from taking further part in the proceedings. The Upper Tribunal confirmed, at [15], that on considering whether to exercise its powers under rule 8 a Tribunal would be required to seek to give effect to the overriding objective set out in rule 2. The Upper Tribunal stated, at [23]: "Striking-out is a draconian remedy of last resort, perhaps especially in an inquisitorial jurisdiction where the participation of both parties is most likely to contribute to achieving the "correct" outcome. Similar rules can be found across many of the Chambers of the First-tier Tribunal, in many of which not only is it common for members of the public to present their own case or to be represented by non-legally qualified people, but for those who represent public bodies also not to have legal qualifications. The tribunals are not intended to be the exclusive preserve of professional lawyers."

Evidence and submissions

The Tribunal has an 'inquisitorial' jurisdiction: see the summary of the relevant body of case law in *A J v. London Borough of Croydon* [2020] UKUT 246 (AAC) at [140]. This means that if there is inadequate information before it about an issue to be determined, it must take the necessary steps to obtain it, if necessary adjourning to do so: *W v. Gloucestershire CC* [2001] EWHC Admin 481 at [15]; see also *R(J) v SENDIST and Brent LBC* [2005] EWHC 3315 at [32]; *MW v Halton BC* [2010] UKUT 34 at [36] and *Birmingham CC v KF* [2018] UKUT 261 (AAC) at [18-19]. In *C v Wiltshire CC* HS/2270/2014 it was held that, where an appellant is unrepresented and there is an evidential shortfall, there may be a duty on the Tribunal to adjourn on its own initiative even if no application for an adjournment has been made. The overarching question a Tribunal must ask itself is whether there is sufficient evidence on which it could properly decide the appeal; if there is, it does not have to perform an inquisitorial function in seeking further evidence, but where there is inadequate information to reach a decision, then it cannot proceed on a purely adversarial basis, but has a duty to act inquisitorially by making sure it has the necessary basic information on which to decide the appeal before it rather than rely entirely on evidence adduced by the parties: *A J v. London Borough of Croydon* at [151].

In addition to its general case management powers in rule 5, under rule 15 the Tribunal may give directions as to the issues on which it requires evidence or submissions; the nature of the evidence or submissions it requires; whether the parties are permitted or required to provide expert evidence, and if so whether the parties must jointly appoint a single expert to provide such evidence; any limit on the number of witnesses whose evidence a party may put forward, whether in relation to a particular issue or generally; the manner in which any evidence or submissions are to be provided, which may include a direction for them to be given orally at a hearing or by written submissions or witness statement; and the time at which any evidence or submissions are to be provided.

The Tribunal has wide powers to admit evidence. Rule 15(2) specifically provides that the Tribunal may admit evidence whether it would be admissible in a civil trial in England and Wales or not, and whether it was available to a previous decision maker or not.

Rule 15(2) also specifically provides that the Tribunal may *exclude* evidence that would otherwise be admissible where the evidence was not provided within the time allowed by a direction or a practice direction or it was otherwise provided in a manner that did not comply with a direction or a practice direction or it would otherwise be unfair to admit the evidence.

In *DH v GH v Staffordshire CC* [2018] UKUT 49 (AAC) parents wanted their child to attend a particular school and called the principal of that school who was also a chartered psychologist but (as told to the Upper Tribunal) was not permitted by the Tribunal to give evidence in the latter capacity in view of his 'financial benefit' in the school. The Upper Tribunal stated, at [48], that a person's financial interest in a school may be a factor to take into account in assessing their evidence but is not of itself a reason for refusing to admit their evidence.

Rule 15(4)(a) gives the Tribunal a specific power to require the parents of the child, or any other person with care of the child or parental responsibility for the child (as defined in section 3 of the Children Act 1989), to make the child available for examination or assessment by a suitably qualified professional person.

Rule 15(4)(b) gives the Tribunal a further specific power to require the person responsible for a school or educational setting to allow a suitably qualified professional person to have access to the school or educational setting for the purpose of assessing the child or the provision made, or to be made, for the child.

Rule 15(5) specifically provides that the Tribunal may consider a failure by a party to comply with a requirement made under rule 15(4), in the absence of any good reason for such failure, as a failure to co-operate with the Tribunal, which could lead to a result which is adverse to that party's case.

In *JS v Worcestershire* [2012] UKUT 451 (AAC) at [20] Mark J stated, "It is trite law that submissions are not evidence and if a representative puts forward alleged facts that are not otherwise in evidence, the tribunal should elicit how far the facts alleged are within his personal knowledge or based on some other evidence that can be produced. Little, if any, weight should normally be attached to assertions by the representative on instructions where there is no other evidence to back up those instructions." However, in *CB v Birmingham City Council* [2018] UKUT 13 (AAC) 13, the Upper Tribunal, having referred to the Tribunal's broad powers to admit evidence under rule 15(2), held that the Tribunal was entitled to accept the local authority's confirmation regarding cost of provision as being factually accurate, stating, "Tribunals are not required to distinguish rigidly between information coming from witnesses and representatives": at [22].

Witnesses and witness summons

Parties are required to notify the Tribunal and each other of the witnesses who will attend the hearing in their Attendance Forms (see further in this Chapter, above).

The SEND Tribunal has published guidance on what witnesses need to do in SEN appeals hearings, which includes the rules for summonsed and expert witnesses. All witnesses should give full, frank and honest evidence and be fair, impartial and independent, even if they are employed or paid by one of the parties.

By rule 15(3), the Tribunal may consent to a witness giving, or require any witness to give, evidence on oath, and may administer an oath for that purpose. In practice, it is rare for witnesses to give evidence on oath in SEN cases.

Rule 16 of the Rules deals with witness summons. On the application of a party or on its own initiative, the Tribunal may summons any person to attend as a witness at a hearing. The summons must give the person required to attend 14 days' notice of the hearing or such shorter period as the Tribunal may direct; and where the person is not a party, make provision for the person's necessary expenses of attendance to be paid, and state who is to pay them. The practice direction states that unless there is a good reason for not doing so a party must make any application for a witness summons at least 14 days before the final hearing.

Expert evidence

The SEND Tribunal guidance on what witnesses need to do in SEN cases sets out that, to be an expert witness, a person must have specialist knowledge about the case, but they do not have to be medically or scientifically qualified. The guidance sets out the matters which a party requesting a person to act as an expert witness should set out in their letter of request, what is expected of expert witnesses and any report they submit as evidence to the Tribunal.

In *RB Kensington & Chelsea v CD* [2015] UKUT 396 at [31-38] the Upper Tribunal gave guidance as to how Tribunals should deal with "non-standard" expert evidence, meaning expert evidence which is not evidence of educational psychology, speech and language therapy and occupational therapy. In that case, the parties had each instructed an acoustic expert to provide a report. As in all cases, the parties and Tribunal must bear in mind the provisions of the overriding objective of rule 2. Further, whilst the Civil Procedure Rules do not apply to the First-tier Tribunal (SEND), and unnecessary formality in those tribunal proceedings must be avoided, nevertheless, Part 35 of the CPR provides a useful backdrop in relation to case management decisions concerning expert evidence in such tribunals. The starting point must be that expert evidence should be restricted to that which is reasonably required to resolve the appeal. If a party intends to seek to rely upon expert evidence, this should be communicated to the other party as soon as possible. If (as is likely in most cases) the issue falls within a substantially established area of knowledge, where it is not necessary for the Tribunal to sample a range of opinion, it may well be that the evidence should be provided by a written report of a single expert jointly instructed by the parties. Any issues regarding expert evidence should be apparent from the parties' respective Attendance Forms. Upon perusal of those Attendance Forms a Tribunal judge may wish to decide whether and, if so, how to exercise their discretion to give directions as to expert evidence. It may well be that the parties would have to make out a strong case either for relying on expert evidence from an expert who had not been jointly instructed, or for requiring oral evidence of an expert at the hearing of the appeal. Further, in giving any case management directions relating to expert evidence, it would be helpful to all involved if the tribunal judge were to identify precisely the issues which the experts are to address.

Late evidence

In *HJ v Brent* [2010] UKUT 15 (AAC) the Tribunal refused to admit late evidence (a video) but did not say why in its written reasons. The Upper Tribunal held, at [13-17], that the Tribunal should have dealt with the late evidence firstly, by considering, as one factor, why the evidence was submitted late and whether it could have been submitted earlier. This is not decisive; it is one factor that has to be taken into account along with any other factor that is relevant to the overriding objective. Logically, the Tribunal should first have decided whether the evidence was relevant. To do so, the Tribunal should have considered what the evidence showed and how that related to the substantive issues on the appeal. In practice, it may not have been possible to decide this question without seeing the video. Other factors included whether the evidence was in dispute anyway and whether the same evidence could be given without the need to view the video. It was also relevant to consider whether the evidence would give rise to satellite issues, such as when the footage was taken, whether it was edited and so on. These factors are not exhaustive. The Tribunal should have taken those and any other relevant factors and, applying the overriding objective, decided whether it was fair and just to exclude the evidence.

The views of the child or young person

Section 19 of the 2014 Act provides that in exercising a function under Part 3 of the 2014 Act in the case of a child or young person, a local authority in England must have regard to, *inter alia* the views, wishes and feelings of the child and his or her parent, or the young person. The Upper Tribunal has decided that this section applies at the appeal stage (*S v Worcestershire County Council* [2017] UKUT 92 (AAC) at [70]; *M and M v West Sussex County Council* [2018] UKUT 347 (AAC) at [40]). Tribunals should, as a matter of routine, deal with the child's views in their reasons: *M and M* at [59]; *BB v London Borough of Barnet* [2019] UKUT 285 at [8]. However, this does not mean that a Tribunal's decision will necessarily be set aside for failing to comply with this duty: *M and M* at [58]; *BB* at [9]. A child's views will not normally be decisive, although they could be: *BB* at [8].

In *West Sussex CC v DN* [2010] UKUT 349 at [33] the Upper Tribunal, having considered *CB v London Borough of Merton and Special Educational Needs Tribunal* [2002] EWHC 877 (Admin) held: "… as a general proposition, it must follow that a local authority would be making an error of law if it totally disregarded the express wishes of a child. Likewise, it would be making an error of law if it followed the views of the child regardless of any countervailing indications that pointed to a different conclusion. It must always be a question of the weight that is to be attached to the views of the child. The older the child and the more mature the child, the greater the weight that should be attached to those views."

In *BB v London Borough of Barnet* there was no evidence of the child's views from the child herself but there was evidence from her mother writing with the experience of seeing her daughter's reactions in different situations, and the Upper Tribunal stated at [9] that it was realistic to treat that as evidence of the child's views in that case.

In *S v Worcestershire* [2017] UKUT 92 at [71-73] Mitchell J held that as this was a case brought by the young person, dealing with it inevitably involved the Tribunal having regard to his views, wishes and feelings. While the Tribunal did not in terms explain why it would not implement his wishes, it explained why it rejected his case which amounted to the same thing. If the Tribunal discharges its obligations under its procedural rules, including the overriding objective, it will be doing as much as would be required if it were subject to the section 19 obligations. Mitchell J stated by way of general guidance that he did not see any need for the Tribunal to complicate its business by expressly seeking to act in accordance with section 19. It should simply act in accordance with the overriding objective and, if it does, will be acting in the spirit of section 19.

Withdrawal of cases and unopposed appeals

A party may give notice of the withdrawal of its case, or any part of it, by sending or delivering to the Tribunal a written notice of withdrawal, or orally at a hearing: rule 17(1). There is a form for this: currently SEND8. However, by rule 17(2), notice of withdrawal will not take effect unless the Tribunal consents to the withdrawal (except where a local authority notifies the Tribunal before the expiry of the time limit for submitting a response that it will not oppose the appeal: rule 17(2)(c)).

A party which has withdrawn its case may apply to the Tribunal for the case to be reinstated: rule 17(4). Such an application must be made in writing and received by the Tribunal within 28 days after the date on which the Tribunal received the withdrawal notice or the date of the hearing at which the case was withdrawn orally: rule 17(5). The Tribunal must notify each party in writing that a withdrawal has taken effect under this rule (rule 17(6)). Where a local authority has notified the Tribunal before the expiry of the time limit for submitting a response that it will not oppose the appeal, the Tribunal's notice under rule 17(6) must also state the date on which the Tribunal was so notified.

Regulation 45 of the 2014 Regulations makes provision for when the local authority notifies the First-tier Tribunal that it will not oppose the appeal before it submits a response. The appeal is to be treated as if it was determined in favour of the appellant and the Tribunal is not required to make an order: regulation 45(2). Regulation 45(3) to (7) sets out what, in law, the LA is then required to do in relation to the different types of appeal. This is addressed further in Chapters 2 to 8 of this book.

Consent orders

The Tribunal may, at the request of the parties *but only if it considers it appropriate*, make a consent order disposing of the proceedings and making such other appropriate provision as the parties have agreed: rule 29. Tribunal need not hold a hearing before making such an order or provide reasons for the order: rule 29(2).

Decisions without a hearing

Tribunal must hold a hearing before making a decision which disposes of proceedings unless each party has consented to the matter being decided without a hearing and the Tribunal considers that it is able to decide the matter without the hearing: rule 23(1). However, the Tribunal may dispose of proceedings without a hearing if it is striking out a party's case under rule 8. In *GA and JA v Wirral MBC (SEN)* [2020] UKUT 24 (AAC) the Upper Tribunal set aside a decision of the First-tier Tribunal which was made without a hearing. The First-tier Tribunal had recorded that the parties had 'agreed' to the matter being decided without a hearing. In fact, the case management directions sent by the Tribunal had required the parties, in effect, to 'opt in' for an oral hearing rather than 'opt out'. The Upper Tribunal held, at [25], that this was not a lawful expression of the legal requirement found in rule 23.

Hearings in a party's absence

If a party fails to attend a hearing the Tribunal may proceed with the hearing if the Tribunal is satisfied that the party has been notified of the hearing or that reasonable steps have been taken to notify the party of the hearing and it considers that it is in the interests of justice to proceed with the hearing: rule 27.

Conduct of the hearing

Appeals are usually listed for a day or half a day depending on the type of appeal (for example, 'BFI' appeals are usually listed for one day, 'refusal to assess' appeals are usually listed for half a day).

The Tribunal 'panel' will comprise a judge of the First-tier Tribunal who will chair the hearing, and a specialist member or members who must have substantial knowledge and experience of working with children and/or young people with SEN and/or disability, and health or social care experience (in extended appeals).

Judges usually conduct appeal hearings in SEN cases in a substantially less formal way than is the case in most other court and tribunal hearings, and the 'format' of hearings can vary considerably.

The Senior President of Tribunals has made a practice direction for the First-tier and Upper Tribunal in relation to "Child, Vulnerable and Sensitive Witnesses". This addresses the circumstances in which such witnesses may be required to give evidence and the manner in which evidence may be given. The practice direction states that a child, vulnerable adult or sensitive witness will only be required to attend as a witness and give evidence at a hearing where the Tribunal determines that the evidence is necessary to enable the fair hearing of the case and their welfare would not be prejudiced by doing so. In practice, it would be very rare for a child or young person to be required to give evidence at a hearing in a SEN case.

The practice direction requires the Tribunal to consider how to facilitate the giving of any evidence by a child, vulnerable adult or sensitive witness and states that it may be appropriate for the Tribunal to direct that the evidence should be given by telephone, video link or other means directed by the Tribunal, or to direct that a person be appointed for the purpose of the hearing who has the appropriate skills or experience in facilitating the giving of evidence by a child, vulnerable adult or sensitive witness.

The Judicial College Equal Treatment Bench Book is also an important document which aims to increase awareness and understanding of the different circumstances of people appearing in courts and tribunals. It suggests steps which should increase participation by all parties.

AA and BA v A Local Authority (SEN) [2021] UKUT 54 (AAC) and *TC and BW v LB Islington* [2021] UKUT 196 (AAC) are cases where the Upper Tribunal considered whether the First-tier Tribunal had done enough to ensure that parties with visual and hearing impairments had a fair hearing.

The President of the Health, Education and Social Care Chamber has issued a presidential guidance note (No. 1 of 2023) on the recording of hearings in the Health, Education and Social Care Chamber and transcription of recordings. This addresses the making of recordings by HMCTS, the prohibition on any party, representative, witness or other member of the press or public recording a hearing without the permission of the Tribunal (which will only be given in exceptional circumstances), access to recordings, transcripts and recording of extemporised judgments.

The expertise of the Tribunal

In *BB v LB Barnet* [2019] UKUT 285, at [15-20], Jacobs J considered the approach the Tribunal should take to using its own expertise. It would be contrary to the overriding objective for a Tribunal to use its special expertise in a way that was inconsistent with dealing with a case fairly and justly, which is another way of saying the parties are entitled to a fair hearing, a common law requirement that is now subsumed, at least in part, by rule 2: at [15]. The ways in which a Tribunal may use its expertise are various, and the circumstances in which they may do so are subject to (possibly infinite) variation; that makes it difficult to establish precise rules, and this, in turn, affects the way that it is appropriate to rely on earlier decisions. They can properly be relied on for statements of principle, but it is wise not to elevate what is really no more than the application of a general principle into a sub-principle or rule: at [16]. The issue is the fairness of the proceeding and fairness depends on the context: at [18]. The parties are under a duty to cooperate under rule 2 of the rules of procedure, and that could mean providing evidence and assisting the Tribunal by inviting the members to put their ideas to the parties and the witnesses: at [18]. As for what the Tribunal should do if something new occurs to the members after the hearing, that depends on what it is that arises. If it is an entirely new issue or basis for decision that no one contemplated during the hearing, fairness will require the Tribunal to put it to the parties. In other cases where the Tribunal's thinking has been effectively, albeit not perhaps directly addressed, putting any new idea to the parties for comment and perhaps more evidence would prolong the proceedings. The Tribunal is entitled to proceed on the basis that the submissions and evidence are complete at the end of the hearing and that further reference back to the parties is not necessary unless something new arises that has not been fairly covered. The Tribunal is entitled to expect the representatives to anticipate the likely range of options that the Tribunal will consider and present their case accordingly: at [18].

Decisions

Regulation 43 of the 2014 Regulations sets out the powers the Tribunal has in determining the different types of appeal under section 51 and regulation 44 sets out the action that the local authority must take in compliance. These regulations are addressed further in Chapters 2 to 9 of this book.

Although, by rule 30(1), the Tribunal may give a decision orally at a hearing, this does not happen in SEN cases where the decision finally disposes of all issues in the proceedings: such decisions are reserved by the Tribunal then sent to the parties in writing, with the Tribunal's reasons for the decision, normally within 10 working days of the final hearing. Rule 30(2) provides that the Tribunal must provide to each party as soon as reasonably practicable after making a decision which finally disposes of all issues in the proceedings, or of a preliminary issue dealt with following a direction under rule 5(3)(e), a decision notice stating the Tribunal's decision, written reasons for the decision, as well as notification of any rights of review or appeal against the decision and the time within which, and the manner in which, such rights of review or appeal may be exercised.

In *H v East Sussex County Council and Others* [2009] EWCA Civ 249 at [14-19] Waller LJ considered the Tribunal's duty to give reasons. He stated that there are dangers in summarising what are suggested to be "requirements" identified in the authorities, as Beatson J was persuaded to do in *R(L) v London Borough of Waltham Forest and Another* [2004] ELR 161 at [14]. Waller LJ stated at [15] that: "the trouble with such a summary is that it risks elevating into general principles what are statements by judges made by reference to the facts and circumstances of particular cases but taken out of context." Waller LJ went on to approve, at [16], the judgment of Sir Thomas Bingham MR in *Meek v Birmingham City Council* [1987] IRLR 250) as the definitive exposition of the attitude superior courts should adopt to the reasons given by Tribunals.

In *SG v Somerset* [2012] UKUT 353 (AAC) at [9] Ward J rejected the submission that one should not have to go behind the Tribunal's decision to other documents in the case in order to reach a true understanding of what was meant by the reasons, in the context of a decision of the First-tier Tribunal in this jurisdiction. The First-tier Tribunal's reasons are not likely to have an extensive readership beyond the immediate parties, and it is the statement of SEN which emerges from the process, rather than the statement of reasons, to which people without knowledge of the litigation are most likely to have occasion to refer. The standard of reasons required was reviewed by the Court of Appeal in *H v East Sussex CC* [2009] EWCA Civ 249, from which it is clear the reasons need to tell the parties why they won or lost and to enable the Upper Tribunal or other appellate body to see whether there has been error of law. The parties will be fully familiar with what has gone on previously. With that knowledge, it will be clear to them what the Tribunal's position was.

Orders for costs

Under rule 10(1) the Tribunal has the power to make an order in respect of costs only under section 29(4) of the Tribunals, Courts and Enforcement Act 2007 and costs incurred in applying for such costs (rule 10(1)(a)), or if the Tribunal considers that a party or its representative has acted "unreasonably in bringing, defending or conducting the proceedings" (rule 10(1)(b)). The reference to section 29(4) of the 2007 Act is to an order that the legal or other representative concerned to meet the whole of any wasted costs or such part of them as may be determined in accordance with Tribunal Procedure Rules. By subsection 27(4) "wasted costs" means any costs incurred by a party as a result of any improper, unreasonable or negligent act or omission on the part of any legal or other representative or any employee of such a representative, or which, in the light of any such act or omission occurring after they were incurred, the relevant Tribunal considers it is unreasonable to expect that party to pay. "Legal or other representative" in this context means any person exercising a right of audience or right to conduct the proceedings on the party's behalf.

The Tribunal may make an order in respect of costs on an application or on its own initiative: rule 10(3). An application may be made at any time during the proceedings but may not be made later than 14 days after the date on which the Tribunal sends a decision notice recording the decision which finally disposes of all issues in the proceedings or notice under rule 17(6) that a withdrawal which ends the proceedings has taken effect: rule 10(5). An application for costs must be made in writing and sent or delivered to the Tribunal and to the person against whom it is proposed that the order be made, together with a schedule of the costs claimed with the application: rule 10(4).

The Tribunal may not make an order for costs without first giving the "paying person" an opportunity to make representations and, if the paying person is an individual, considering that person's financial means: rule 10(6).

The amount of costs to be paid under the order may be ascertained by summary assessment by the Tribunal, agreement of a specified sum by the 'paying person' and the 'receiving person' or assessment of the whole or a specified part of the costs, including the costs of the assessment, incurred by the receiving person, if not agreed: rule 10(7). If there is an order for assessment under rule 10(7)(c), the paying person or the receiving person may apply to a county court for a detailed assessment of costs in accordance with the Civil Procedure Rules 1998 on the standard basis or, if specified in the order, on the indemnity basis. Upon making an order for the assessment of costs, the Tribunal may order an amount to be paid on account before the costs or expenses are assessed: rule 10(8).

In *HJ v London Borough of Brent* [2011] UKUT 191 (AAC) at [7-13] the Upper Tribunal considered the relevant case law. The meaning of 'unreasonable' was discussed by the Court of Appeal in *Ridehalgh v Horsefield* [1994] Ch 205 at 232 in the context of wasted costs. The Court of Appeal considered an equivalent provision to rule 10(1)(b) in *McPherson v BNP Paribas (London Branch)* [2004] ICR 1398 which concerned a claim before an employment tribunal which the claimant had withdrawn. Mummery LJ discussed a number of points of general relevance. First, at [30], the question was whether, in all the circumstances of the case, the claimant in withdrawing his claim had conducted the proceedings reasonably, not whether the withdrawal of the claim was in itself reasonable. Second, at [40], the costs that may be awarded are not limited to those that are attributable to the unreasonable conduct: the tribunal must have regard to the nature, gravity and effect of the unreasonable conduct as factors relevant to the exercise of the discretion whether to order costs, but that is not the same as requiring the receiving party to prove that specific unreasonable conduct by the paying party caused particular costs to be incurred. Third, at [41], costs must not be punitive, in that the indemnity principle should not apply to the award of costs, but it is not punitive and impermissible for a tribunal to order costs without confining them to the costs attributable to the unreasonable conduct. Fourth, at [41], the unreasonable conduct is relevant at three stages: it is a precondition to order costs and it is also a relevant factor to be taken into account in deciding whether to make an order for costs and the form of the order. *Kovacs v Queen Mary and Westfield College* [2002] ICR 919 was also considered. In *HJ v London Borough of Brent* the Upper Tribunal declined to award costs, stating, at [17], "In making my assessment, it is not proper to second guess a party's decisions in the course of litigation. Merely because particular evidence in the end secured a particular outcome, it does not follow that it was unreasonable to defend the case or that it was unreasonably conducted... The reasonableness of a party's conduct has to take into account the ongoing and evolving nature of the proceedings."

In *MG v Cambridgeshire County Council* [2017] UKUT 172 (AAC) at [26-27] Rowley J discouraged applications for costs, stating, "The general rule in this jurisdiction is that there should be no order as to costs. There are good and obvious reasons for the rule. Tribunal proceedings should be as brief, straightforward and informal as possible. And it is crucial that parties should not be deterred from bringing or defending appeals through fear of an application for costs… Furthermore, tribunals should apply considerable restraint when considering an application under rule 10, and should make an order only in the most obvious cases. In other words, an order for costs will be very much the exception rather than the rule."

CHAPTER ELEVEN

CORRECTING, SETTING ASIDE, REVIEWING AND APPEALING FIRST-TIER TRIBUNAL DECISIONS

Overview

Sections 9 to 12 of the Tribunals, Courts and Enforcement Act 2007 make provision for reviews and appeals of decisions of the First-tier Tribunal. Part 5 of The Tribunal Procedure (First-tier Tribunal) (Health, Education and Social Care Chamber) Rules 2008, rules 43-50, deal with correcting, setting aside, reviewing and appealing First-tier Tribunal decisions. Procedure in the Upper Tribunal is governed by The Tribunal Procedure (Upper Tribunal) Rules 2008.

By Rule 50 of the FTT Procedure Rules, the First-tier Tribunal may treat an application for a decision to be corrected, set aside or reviewed, or for permission to appeal against a decision, as an application for any other one of those things.

Under rule 5(3)(l) of the FTT Procedure Rules, the First-tier Tribunal can suspend the effect of its own decision pending the determination by the Tribunal or the Upper Tribunal of an application for permission to appeal against, and any appeal or review of, that decision.

Clerical mistakes and accidental slips or omissions

These are provided for by rule 44 of the FTT Procedure Rules. The Tribunal may at any time correct any clerical mistake or other accidental slip or omission in a decision, direction or any document produced by it, by (a) sending notification of the amended decision or direction, or a copy of the amended document, to all parties; and (b) making any necessary amendment to any information published in relation to the decision, direction or document.

Setting aside a decision which disposes of proceedings

By rule 45 of the FTT Procedure Rules, the Tribunal may set aside a decision which disposes of proceedings, or part of such a decision, and re-make the decision or the relevant part of it. The circumstances in which it may do so are set out at rule 45(1) and (2): (a) the Tribunal considers that it is in the interests of justice to do so; and (b) one or more of the conditions in rule 4(2) are satisfied. These are: (a) a document relating to the proceedings was not sent to, or was not received at an appropriate time by, a party or a party's representative; (b) a document relating to the proceedings was not sent to the Tribunal at an appropriate time; (c) a party, or a party's representative, was not present at a hearing related to the proceedings; or (d) there has been some other procedural irregularity in the proceedings.

By rule 45(3), a party applying for a decision, or part of a decision, to be set aside under Rule 45 must make a written application to the Tribunal so that it is received no later than 28 days after the date on which the Tribunal sent notice of the decision to the party.

Review of a decision

"Review" for the purposes of Part 5 of the Procedure Rules means the review of a decision by the Tribunal under section 9 of the Tribunals, Courts and Enforcement Act 2007: rule 43 of the FTT Procedure Rules. By section 9(1) of the 2007 Act, the First-tier Tribunal may review a decision made by it on a matter in a case, but there are provisions in sections 9 and 11 of the 2007 Act which, in broad terms, prevent it from endlessly reviewing reviews. These provisions are explained further in this section, below.

By rule 49(1) of the FTT Procedure Rules, the Tribunal may only undertake a review of a decision in two situations. The first situation is pursuant to rule 47(1), which requires the Tribunal, upon receiving an application for permission to appeal, first to consider, taking into account the overriding objective in rule 2, whether to review the decision in accordance with rule 49. The Tribunal may review a decision pursuant to rule 47(1) if it is satisfied that there was an error of law in the decision: rule 49(1)(a). The procedure for this type of review is explained in more detail in the section on rule 47(1) reviews, below. The second situation is pursuant to rule 48, which specifically applies to decisions which dispose of proceedings in SEN cases. By rule 48(2) a party may make a written application to the Tribunal for a review of a decision "if circumstances relevant to the decision have changed since the decision was made." The procedure for this type of review is explained in more detail in the section on rule 48 reviews, below.

By rule 49(2) of the First-tier Tribunal Procedure Rules, the Tribunal must notify the parties in writing of the outcome of any review, and of any right of appeal in relation to the outcome. By rule 48(3), if the Tribunal takes any action in relation to a decision following a review without first giving every party an opportunity to make representations, then the notice given under rule 49(2) must state that any party that did not have an opportunity to make representations may apply for such action to be set aside and for the decision to be reviewed again.

By section 9(4) of the 2007 Act, where the First-tier Tribunal has reviewed a decision, it may, in the light of the review, do any of the following: (a) correct accidental errors in the decision or in a record of the decision; (b) amend reasons given for the decision; (c) set the decision aside. By section 9(5), if the First-tier Tribunal sets a decision aside, it has two alternatives. The first is that it must re-decide the matter concerned. The second is that it must refer that matter to the Upper Tribunal. By section 9(8), if the First-tier Tribunal is re-deciding the matter, it may make such findings of fact as it considers appropriate.

By sections 9(6) and 9(7), where a matter is referred to the Upper Tribunal under section 9(5)(b), the Upper Tribunal must re-decide the matter, and in so-doing, it may make any decision which the First-tier Tribunal could make if the First-tier Tribunal were re-deciding the matter. By section 9(8), it may also make such findings of fact as it considers appropriate. Rule 26A of the Upper Tribunal Procedure Rules makes provision for cases referred to the Upper Tribunal from the First-tier Tribunal. The Upper Tribunal must give directions as to the procedure to be followed in the consideration and disposal of the proceedings.

By section 9(10), a decision of the First-tier Tribunal may not be reviewed under section 9(1) more than once, and once the First-tier Tribunal has decided that an earlier decision should not be reviewed under section 9(1) it may not then decide to review that earlier decision under that subsection. However, by section 9(11), where under section 9 a decision is set aside and the matter concerned is then re-decided, the decision set aside and the decision made in re-deciding the matter are for the purposes of section 9(10) to be taken to be different decisions.

In the context of an appeal under section 51 of the Children and Families Act 2014, an "excluded decision" for the purposes of section 11(1) will be a decision under section 11(5)(d) or (e), that is: a decision of the First-tier Tribunal under section 9 of the 2007 Act: (i) to review, or not to review, an earlier decision of the Tribunal, (ii) to take no action, or not to take any particular action, in the light of a review of an earlier decision of the Tribunal, (iii) to set aside an earlier decision of the Tribunal, or (iv) to refer, or not to refer, a matter to the Upper Tribunal; or a decision of the First-tier Tribunal that is set aside under section 9 (including a decision set aside after proceedings on an appeal have been begun). By section 9(9), a decision under section 9(4)(c) to set aside an earlier decision of the Tribunal may be reviewed under section 9(1), but the First-tier Tribunal's only power in the light of such a review is the power under section 9(4)(a) to correct accidental errors in the decision or in a record of the decision.

Reviews pursuant to section 47(1)

By rule 47(1) of the FTT Procedure Rules, the First-tier Tribunal, on receiving an application for permission to appeal, must first consider, taking into account the overriding objective in rule 2, whether to review the decision in accordance with rule 49 (review of a decision). The law and FTT Procedure Rules relating to applications for permission to appeal are explained further in the section on appeals, below. By rule 49(1) of the FTT Procedure Rules, the Tribunal may only undertake a review of a decision pursuant to rule 47(1) if it is satisfied that there was an error of law in the decision. If the Tribunal decides not to review the decision, or reviews the decision and decides to take no action in relation to the decision, or part of it, it must consider whether to give permission to appeal in relation to the decision or that part of it: rule 47(2). By rule 47(3), the Tribunal must send a record of its decision to the parties as soon as practicable.

The law and Procedure Rules relating to the First-tier Tribunal's consideration of an application for permission to appeal are explained further in the section on appeals, below.

Reviews pursuant to section 48

By rule 48(2) of the FTT Tribunal Procedure Rules, a party may make a written application to the First-tier Tribunal for a review of a decision "if circumstances relevant to the decision have changed since the decision was made."

By rule 48(3), such an application must be sent or delivered to the Tribunal so that it is received within 28 days after the date on which the Tribunal sent the decision notice recording the Tribunal's decision to the party making the application. Rule 48(4) makes provision for late applications for a review. The Tribunal has a case management power under rule 5(3)(a) to extend the time limit within which the application must have been received. However, if a party applies for a review outside of the 28-day time limit, or outside of any extension to the time limit which the Tribunal has given, then the application must include a request for an extension of time and the reason why the application was not provided in time: rule 48(4)(a). Unless the Tribunal extends time for the application under rule 5(3)(a) then, by rule 48(4)(b), the Tribunal must not admit the application.

Consistent with the provisions in sections 9 and 11 of the 2007 Act in relation to "excluded decisions", rule 48 applies to decisions which dispose of proceedings in SEN cases, but not to decisions under Part 5 of the FTT Procedure Rules: rule 48(1).

Appeal of a decision

For the purposes of Part 5 of the FTT Procedure Rules, "appeal" means the exercise of a right of appeal to the Upper Tribunal on any point of law arising from a decision made by the First-tier Tribunal other than an excluded decision under section 11 of the Tribunals, Courts and Enforcement Act 2007: rule 43.

In the context of an appeal under section 51 of the Children and Families Act 2014, an "excluded decision" for the purposes of section 11(1) of the 2007 Act will be a decision under section 11(5)(d) or (e), that is: a decision of the First-tier Tribunal under section 9 of the 2007 Act: (i) to review, or not to review, an earlier decision of the Tribunal, (ii) to take no action, or not to take any particular action, in the light of a review of an earlier decision of the Tribunal, (iii) to set aside an earlier decision of the Tribunal, or (iv) to refer, or not to refer, a matter to the Upper Tribunal; or a decision of the First-tier Tribunal that is set aside under section 9 (including a decision set aside after proceedings on an appeal have been begun).

Any party to an appeal under section 51 of the 2014 Act has a right of appeal. However, that right may be exercised only with permission (or leave), which may be given by (a) the First-tier Tribunal, or (b) the Upper Tribunal on an application by the party: sections 11(2), (3) and (4) of the 2007 Act.

The first step for a party who wishes to appeal a decision of the First-tier Tribunal is to make a written application to the First-tier Tribunal for permission to appeal: rule 46(1) of the FTT Procedure Rules.

By rule 46(2) of the FTT Procedure Rules, the application must be sent or delivered to the First-tier Tribunal so that it is received no later than 28 days after the latest of the dates that the Tribunal sends to the person making the application: the relevant decision notice (42(2)(za)); written reasons for the decision, if the decision disposes of all issues in the proceedings (42(2)(a)(i)); written reasons for the decision, if the decision disposes of a preliminary issue dealt with following a direction under rule 5(3)(e) (this is subject to rule 46(2A), under which the Tribunal may direct that the 28-day time limit shall run from the date of the decision that disposes of all issues in the proceedings) (42(2)(a)(ii)); notification of amended reasons for, or correction of, the decision following a review (42(2)(b)); or notification that an application for the decision to be set aside has been unsuccessful (42(2)(c)). The date in 42(2)(c) applies only if the application for the decision to be set aside was made within the time stipulated in rule 45 (setting aside a decision which disposes of proceedings) or any extension of that time granted by the Tribunal.

Rule 46(4) makes provision for late applications to the First-tier Tribunal for permission to appeal. The Tribunal has a case management power under rule 5(3)(a) of the FTT Procedure Rules to extend the time limit within which the application must have been received. However, if a party applies for a review outside of the 28-day time limit, or outside of any extension to the time limit which the Tribunal has given, then the application must include a request for an extension of time and the reason why the application was not provided in time: rule 46(4)(a). Unless the Tribunal extends time for the application under rule 5(3)(a) then, by rule 46(4)(b), the Tribunal must not admit the application.

By rule 46(5) an application for permission to appeal must identify the decision of the First-tier Tribunal to which it relates, the alleged error or errors of law in the decision and state the result the party making the application is seeking.

As set out above, by rule 47(1) of the FTT Procedure Rules, on receiving an application for permission to appeal the First-tier Tribunal must first consider whether to review the decision in accordance with rule 49, and if it decides not to review the decision, or reviews the decision and decides to take no action in relation to the decision, or part of it, it must consider whether to give permission to appeal in relation to the decision or that part of it: rule 47(2). The Tribunal must send a record of its decision to the parties as soon as practicable: rule 47(3).

If the First-tier Tribunal refuses permission to appeal it must send with the record of its decision a statement of its reasons for such refusal and notification of the right to make an application to the Upper Tribunal for permission to appeal and the time within which, and the method by which, such application must be made: rule 47(4). The First-tier Tribunal may give permission to appeal on limited grounds but must comply with rule 47(4) in relation to any grounds on which it has refused permission.

If First-tier Tribunal refuses the application for permission to appeal or does not admit it or grants it only on limited grounds, the next step for the party who wants to appeal is to apply to the Upper Tribunal for permission to appeal to the Upper Tribunal under rule 21 of the UT Procedure Rules.

In the context of an appeal under 51 of the 2014 Act, i.e. in SEN cases, rule 21(3)(b) of the UT Procedure Rules provides that an application for permission to appeal must be made in writing and received by the Upper Tribunal no later than a month after the date on which the First-tier Tribunal sent notice of its refusal of permission to appeal (which, by rule 21(8) includes a notice of a grant of permission to appeal on limited grounds) or refusal to admit the application for permission to appeal, to the appellant.

Rules 21(6) and 21(7) of the UT Procedure Rules make provision for late applications for permission to appeal to the Upper Tribunal. The Upper Tribunal has a case management power under rule 5(3)(a) of the UT Procedure Rules to extend the time limit within which the application must have been received. However, if a party applies to the Upper Tribunal for permission to appeal outside of the one-month time limit, or outside of any extension to the time limit which the Upper Tribunal has given, then the application must include a request for an extension of time and the reason why the application was not provided in time: rule 28(3)(a). Unless the Upper Tribunal extends time for the application under rule 5(3)(a) then, by rule 21(3)(b), the Upper Tribunal must not admit the application. By rule 21(7) of the UT Procedure Rules, if the First-tier Tribunal refused to admit the appellant's application for permission to appeal because it was not made in time, the application to the Upper Tribunal for permission to appeal must include the reason why the application to the First-tier tribunal was not made in time and the Upper Tribunal must only admit the application if it considers that it is in the interests of justice for it to do so.

Rule 21 of the UT Procedure Rules sets out the further procedural requirements relating to the application to the Upper Tribunal for permission to appeal and rule 22 sets out the Upper Tribunal's procedure for deciding that application. Rule 23 addresses the procedural requirements in relation to the notice of appeal where the Upper Tribunal has given permission to appeal and has given a direction that the application for permission to appeal does not stand as the notice of appeal. Rule 24 sets out the procedural requirements in relation to the response to the appeal and rule 25 makes provision for an appellant's reply. The Upper Tribunal's general and specific case management powers are set out in Part 2 of the UT Procedure Rules, including rule 12 on calculating time. Part 5 deals with hearings, Part 6 with decisions, and Part 7 with correcting, setting aside, reviewing and appealing decisions of the Upper Tribunal.

By rule 5(3)(m) of the UT Procedure Rules, in an appeal, or an application for permission to appeal, against the decision of the First-tier Tribunal, the Upper Tribunal has a power to suspend the effect of that decision pending the determination of the application for permission to appeal, and any appeal.

By section 12 of the Tribunals, Courts and Enforcement Act 2007, if the Upper Tribunal finds that the making of the decision concerned involved the making of an error on a point of law the Upper Tribunal may (but need not) set aside the decision of the First-tier Tribunal. If it does, it must either remit the case to the First-tier Tribunal with directions for its reconsideration or re-make the decision. In remitting the case to the First-tier Tribunal with directions for its reconsideration, the Upper Tribunal may also direct that the members of the First-tier Tribunal who are chosen to reconsider the case are not to be the same as those who made the decision that has been set aside; and give procedural directions in connection with the reconsideration of the case by the First-tier Tribunal. In re-making the decision, the Upper Tribunal may make any decision which the First-tier Tribunal could make if the First-tier Tribunal were re-making the decision and may make such findings of fact as it considers appropriate.

MORE BOOKS BY LAW BRIEF PUBLISHING

A selection of our other titles available now:-

'A Practical Guide to Parental Alienation in Private and Public Law Children Cases' by Sam King QC & Frankie Shama
'Contested Heritage – Removing Art from Land and Historic Buildings' by Richard Harwood QC, Catherine Dobson, David Sawtell
'The Limits of Separate Legal Personality: When Those Running a Company Can Be Held Personally Liable for Losses Caused to Third Parties Outside of the Company' by Dr Mike Wilkinson
'A Practical Guide to Transgender Law' by Robin Moira White & Nicola Newbegin
'Artificial Intelligence – The Practical Legal Issues (2nd Edition)' by John Buyers
'A Practical Guide to Residential Freehold Conveyancing' by Lorraine Richardson
'A Practical Guide to Pensions on Divorce for Lawyers' by Bryan Scant
'A Practical Guide to Challenging Sham Marriage Allegations in Immigration Law' by Priya Solanki
'A Practical Guide to Legal Rights in Scotland' by Sarah-Jane Macdonald
'A Practical Guide to New Build Conveyancing' by Paul Sams & Rebecca East
'A Practical Guide to Defending Barristers in Disciplinary Cases' by Marc Beaumont
'A Practical Guide to Inherited Wealth on Divorce' by Hayley Trim
'A Practical Guide to Practice Direction 12J and Domestic Abuse in Private Law Children Proceedings' by Rebecca Cross & Malvika Jaganmohan
'A Practical Guide to Confiscation and Restraint' by Narita Bahra QC, John Carl Townsend, David Winch
'A Practical Guide to the Law of Forests in Scotland' by Philip Buchan
'A Practical Guide to Health and Medical Cases in Immigration Law' by Rebecca Chapman & Miranda Butler
'A Practical Guide to Bad Character Evidence for Criminal Practitioners by Aparna Rao
'A Practical Guide to Extradition Law post-Brexit' by Myles Grandison et al

'A Practical Guide to Hoarding and Mental Health for Housing Lawyers' by Rachel Coyle
'A Practical Guide to Psychiatric Claims in Personal Injury – 2nd Edition' by Liam Ryan
'Stephens on Contractual Indemnities' by Richard Stephens
'A Practical Guide to the EU Succession Regulation' by Richard Frimston
'A Practical Guide to Solicitor and Client Costs – 2nd Edition' by Robin Dunne
'Constructive Dismissal – Practice Pointers and Principles' by Benjimin Burgher
'A Practical Guide to Religion and Belief Discrimination Claims in the Workplace' by Kashif Ali
'A Practical Guide to the Law of Medical Treatment Decisions' by Ben Troke
'Fundamental Dishonesty and QOCS in Personal Injury Proceedings: Law and Practice' by Jake Rowley
'A Practical Guide to the Law in Relation to School Exclusions' by Charlotte Hadfield & Alice de Coverley
'A Practical Guide to Divorce for the Silver Separators' by Karin Walker
'The Right to be Forgotten – The Law and Practical Issues' by Melissa Stock
'A Practical Guide to Planning Law and Rights of Way in National Parks, the Broads and AONBs' by James Maurici QC, James Neill et al
'A Practical Guide to Election Law' by Tom Tabori
'A Practical Guide to the Law in Relation to Surrogacy' by Andrew Powell
'A Practical Guide to Claims Arising from Fatal Accidents – 2nd Edition' by James Patience
'A Practical Guide to the Ownership of Employee Inventions – From Entitlement to Compensation' by James Tumbridge & Ashley Roughton
'A Practical Guide to Asbestos Claims' by Jonathan Owen & Gareth McAloon
'A Practical Guide to Stamp Duty Land Tax in England and Northern Ireland' by Suzanne O'Hara
'A Practical Guide to the Law of Farming Partnerships' by Philip Whitcomb
'Covid-19, Homeworking and the Law – The Essential Guide to Employment and GDPR Issues' by Forbes Solicitors
'Covid-19 and Criminal Law – The Essential Guide' by Ramya Nagesh
'Covid-19 and Family Law in England and Wales – The Essential Guide' by Safda Mahmood

'A Practical Guide to the Law of Unlawful Eviction and Harassment – 2nd Edition' by Stephanie Lovegrove
'Covid-19, Brexit and the Law of Commercial Leases – The Essential Guide' by Mark Shelton
'A Practical Guide to Costs in Personal Injury Claims – 2nd Edition' by Matthew Hoe
'A Practical Guide to the General Data Protection Regulation (GDPR) – 2nd Edition' by Keith Markham
'Ellis on Credit Hire – Sixth Edition' by Aidan Ellis & Tim Kevan
'A Practical Guide to Working with Litigants in Person and McKenzie Friends in Family Cases' by Stuart Barlow
'Protecting Unregistered Brands: A Practical Guide to the Law of Passing Off' by Lorna Brazell
'A Practical Guide to Secondary Liability and Joint Enterprise Post-Jogee' by Joanne Cecil & James Mehigan
'A Practical Guide to the Pre-Action RTA Claims Protocol for Personal Injury Lawyers' by Antonia Ford
'A Practical Guide to Neighbour Disputes and the Law' by Alexander Walsh
'A Practical Guide to Forfeiture of Leases' by Mark Shelton
'A Practical Guide to Coercive Control for Legal Practitioners and Victims' by Rachel Horman
'A Practical Guide to Rights Over Airspace and Subsoil' by Daniel Gatty
'Tackling Disclosure in the Criminal Courts – A Practitioner's Guide' by Narita Bahra QC & Don Ramble
'A Practical Guide to the Law of Driverless Cars – Second Edition' by Alex Glassbrook, Emma Northey & Scarlett Milligan
'A Practical Guide to TOLATA Claims' by Greg Williams
'A Practical Guide to Elderly Law – 2nd Edition' by Justin Patten
'A Practical Guide to Responding to Housing Disrepair and Unfitness Claims' by Iain Wightwick
'A Practical Guide to the Construction and Rectification of Wills and Trust Instruments' by Edward Hewitt
'A Practical Guide to the Law of Bullying and Harassment in the Workplace' by Philip Hyland
'How to Be a Freelance Solicitor: A Practical Guide to the SRA-Regulated Freelance Solicitor Model' by Paul Bennett

'A Practical Guide to Prison Injury Claims' by Malcolm Johnson
'A Practical Guide to the Small Claims Track - 2nd Edition' by Dominic Bright
'A Practical Guide to Advising Clients at the Police Station' by Colin Stephen McKeown-Beaumont
'A Practical Guide to Antisocial Behaviour Injunctions' by Iain Wightwick
'Practical Mediation: A Guide for Mediators, Advocates, Advisers, Lawyers, and Students in Civil, Commercial, Business, Property, Workplace, and Employment Cases' by Jonathan Dingle with John Sephton
'The Mini-Pupillage Workbook' by David Boyle
'A Practical Guide to Crofting Law' by Brian Inkster
'A Practical Guide to Spousal Maintenance' by Liz Cowell
'A Practical Guide to the Law of Domain Names and Cybersquatting' by Andrew Clemson
'A Practical Guide to the Law of Gender Pay Gap Reporting' by Harini Iyengar
'A Practical Guide to the Rights of Grandparents in Children Proceedings' by Stuart Barlow
'NHS Whistleblowing and the Law' by Joseph England
'Employment Law and the Gig Economy' by Nigel Mackay & Annie Powell
'A Practical Guide to Noise Induced Hearing Loss (NIHL) Claims' by Andrew Mckie, Ian Skeate, Gareth McAloon
'An Introduction to Beauty Negligence Claims – A Practical Guide for the Personal Injury Practitioner' by Greg Almond
'Intercompany Agreements for Transfer Pricing Compliance' by Paul Sutton
'Zen and the Art of Mediation' by Martin Plowman
'A Practical Guide to the SRA Principles, Individual and Law Firm Codes of Conduct 2019 – What Every Law Firm Needs to Know' by Paul Bennett
'A Practical Guide to Adoption for Family Lawyers' by Graham Pegg
'A Practical Guide to Industrial Disease Claims' by Andrew Mckie & Ian Skeate
'A Practical Guide to Redundancy' by Philip Hyland
'A Practical Guide to Vicarious Liability' by Mariel Irvine
'A Practical Guide to Applications for Landlord's Consent and Variation of Leases' by Mark Shelton
'A Practical Guide to Relief from Sanctions Post-Mitchell and Denton' by Peter Causton

www.ingramcontent.com/pod-product-compliance
Lightning Source LLC
LaVergne TN
LVHW052324200926
848481LV00002B/660
* 9 7 8 1 9 1 3 7 1 5 3 4 2 *